These essays are an appraisal of the critical first year of the Alliance for Progress—genesis, achievement, outlook—by five distinguished statesmen:

Milton S. Eisenhower
President of The Johns Hopkins University, formerly Special Ambassador to Latin America.

Raúl Prebisch
Under Secretary of the United Nations in Charge of the Economic Commission for Latin America.

José Figueres
Leader of the 1948 revolution in Costa Rica, later president of that country.

Teodoro Moscoso
U. S. Coordinator of the Alliance for Progress.

Dean Rusk
Secretary of State of the United States.

The Alliance for Progress was created to stimulate economic, social, and political development among the Latin American nations. It has as its fundamental purpose the alleviation of

(continued on back flap)

enlightened public opinion and support which are essential to the success of the new Alliance.

THE ALLIANCE FOR PROGRESS:
PROBLEMS AND PERSPECTIVES

Books on Foreign Affairs from
The Johns Hopkins University
School of Advanced International Studies

Southeast Asia in the Coming World, Philip W. Thayer, ed.

The Threat of Soviet Imperialism, C. Grove Haines, ed.

Africa Today, C. Grove Haines, ed.

Nationalism and Progress in Free Asia, Philip W. Thayer, ed.

Tensions in the Middle East, Philip W. Thayer, ed.

War and Peace in the Law of Islam, Majid Khadduri

European Integration, C. Grove Haines, ed.

Alliance Policy in the Cold War, Arnold Wolfers, ed.

Islamic Jurisprudence: Shāfi'ī's Risāla, Trans. and with an Introduction by Majid Khadduri

The United States and the United Nations, Francis O. Wilcox and H. Field Haviland, Jr., eds.

Nations in Alliance: The Limits of Interdependence, George Liska

Discord and Collaboration: Essays on International Politics, Arnold Wolfers

The Alliance for Progress: Problems and Perspectives, John C. Dreier, ed.

THE ALLIANCE FOR PROGRESS
Problems and Perspectives

Edited by John C. Dreier

The Johns Hopkins Press: Baltimore

© 1962, The Johns Hopkins Press, Baltimore 18, Maryland
Distributed in Great Britain by Oxford University Press, London
Printed in the United States of America
Library of Congress Catalog Card Number 62–18508
Second Printing, 1963

FOREWORD

The School of Advanced International Studies, of The Johns Hopkins University, was pleased to be able to sponsor this series of lectures in the nation's capital on the Alliance for Progress. Any doubt about the interest of the American people in the Alliance was completely dispelled by the overflow crowds which attended each of the five lectures in the Pan American Union's historic Hall of the Americas.

Personally, I have never labored under any illusion about the willingness of our people to extend long-range aid to the people of Latin America. Ten years' experience on Capitol Hill convinced me that the Latin American segment of our foreign aid programs was far more popular than any other part of the mutual assistance bill. Often senators and congressmen actively interested in reducing the amount of aid going to Europe, Asia, and Africa would take the lead in supporting amendments designed to increase our assistance to the other Americas.

In this connection, it should be reassuring to our Latin American friends that the program now incorporated in the Alliance has such strong bipartisan support in this country. Since it was started during the Eisenhower administration, and developed and broadened during the Kennedy administration, it would be difficult indeed for either Republicans or Democrats to disown it. The prospects for continuing support over a long period of time are exceptionally bright.

This is not to say that the United States will be behind the program regardless of what may happen. Our people will gladly carry our share of the Alliance burden as long as they are convinced that their sacrifices are, in fact, promoting social justice in the Americas. But they will not be willing to pour large amounts of aid into Latin America unless they can be assured it will bring commensurate results in bettering the lot of the common man and not just feathering the nests of the privileged few.

When Frederick the Great was shown the peace plan of the Abbe St. Pierre, he is said to have praised it as an excellent plan. "All we need now," he said, "is the consent of Europe and a few similar trifles." Although the parallel may not be an exact one, it is clear that the last great requirement now for the success of the Alliance is its complete acceptance by the leaders and the people of Latin America. By this I mean far more than just mere lip service to great ideals; I mean a willingness and a determination to take those steps necessary—and some of them will be exceedingly painful—to bring the Alliance into full fruition.

Time, of course, is of the utmost importance. Social and economic progress almost always comes slowly, and if we try to move too fast we could defeat our purpose. On the other hand, if we proceed too slowly we may never come in sight of our great goal.

Latin America will be watching the United States to see if we move ahead quickly enough in formulating the policies and taking the necessary actions to administer our part of the program effectively.

We will be watching our good neighbors just as intently to see how quickly they take the first meaningful steps in the direction of the social, political, and economic reforms which they agree are essential to the success of the Alliance.

FOREWORD

And the whole world will be watching us all to see whether, through our joint efforts, the relatively slow tempo of development in the Americas can be accelerated sufficiently so that the hopes and aspirations of the people of Latin America may be realized in an atmosphere of freedom and progress.

The program of lectures included in this volume was arranged by the Inter-American Center, of the School of Advanced International Studies, under the direction of John C. Dreier, formerly our Ambassador on the Council of the Organization of American States. The topics were selected to give a broad perspective of the entire Alliance. The lecturers were chosen from among the ablest authorities both in the United States and Latin America, as evidenced by the excellence of their contributions. We hope that the discussions stimulated by this program in Washington, together with the published volumes now appearing in both English and Spanish, will be of real value to the people and the leaders of the New World in meeting the challenge that lies ahead.

The School of Advanced International Studies would like to express its appreciation to the Westinghouse Electric International Company for its generous support of the lecture series. We wish also to thank the Friends of the United States of Latin America and the Pan American Union for their valuable collaboration toward the successful execution of this program.

Francis O. Wilcox, Dean
School of Advanced International Studies
The Johns Hopkins University

CONTENTS

Foreword, Francis O. Wilcox v

The Contributors x

Editor's Introduction xiii

1. THE ALLIANCE FOR PROGRESS: HISTORIC ROOTS
   Milton S. Eisenhower 1

2. ECONOMIC ASPECTS OF THE ALLIANCE
   Raúl Prebisch 24

3. THE ALLIANCE AND POLITICAL GOALS
   José Figueres 66

4. SOCIAL CHANGE AND THE ALLIANCE
   Teodoro Moscoso 89

5. THE ALLIANCE IN THE CONTEXT OF WORLD AFFAIRS
   Dean Rusk 102

The Charter of Punta del Este 118

Index 142

THE CONTRIBUTORS

MILTON S. EISENHOWER has been actively concerned with Latin American relations for many years. As Special Ambassador and Personal Representative of the President of the United States, he made several visits to Latin America from 1953 to 1960. His major study trips resulted in the publication in 1953 and 1958 of two reports on "United States-Latin American Relations" in which he examined and made recommendations regarding United States policies and programs in the area. In 1956-57, Dr. Eisenhower served as United States member and chairman of the Inter-American Committee of Presidential Representatives which formulated a series of recommendations for strengthening cooperation among the American Republics in the economic and social fields, and in 1959-60 he served as a member of the National Advisory Committee on Inter-American Affairs. Having served twenty years in the field of higher education, Dr. Eisenhower is now president of The Johns Hopkins University.

RAÚL PREBISCH now occupies a dual role symbolizing his broad personal contribution to inter-American economic relations. As Under-Secretary of the United Nations in Charge of the Economic Commission for Latin America, Dr. Prebisch has directed the preparation of a series of challenging reports analyzing Latin America's economic position in the world and advocating policies aimed at the economic development of the region. Now, as Coordinator for the Panel of Experts of the Organization of American States, he is playing a major part in the task entrusted to this group of advising governments with respect to their national plans for economic development under the Alliance for Progress. He brings to this task not only many years of public service, but a distinguished academic career in the course of which he has held many professorships in economics and received numerous academic honors both in his native Argentina and elsewhere.

THE CONTRIBUTORS

JOSÉ FIGUERES is well known in both the United States and Latin America for his vigorous espousal of democratic principles and equally strong antipathy to dictatorships of the right or left. After leading the revolution of 1948, Mr. Figueres became provisional president of Costa Rica until constitutional government was restored and a popularly elected administration installed. In 1953, Mr. Figueres himself ran for the presidency and was elected. While not at present holding public office, he continues to display an active and articulate interest in national and international affairs. Among other recent activities, Mr. Figueres has promoted the establishment in Costa Rica of the Institute of Political Education, where young men and women from several Latin American countries come for intensive training in progressive, democratic political action programs.

TEODORO MOSCOSO has a long record of achievement as an administrator of economic development programs. Born in Spain, Mr. Moscoso grew up in Ponce, Puerto Rico. He graduated from the University of Michigan in 1932. After a period of several years in the family drug business, he started his career in public affairs with the Ponce Municipal Housing Authority. A principal member of the group of men surrounding Governor Luis Muñoz Marín who were responsible for the execution of "Operation Bootstrap," Mr. Moscoso became the first President of the Puerto Rico Industrial Development Company, and of the subsequently established Puerto Rican Economic Development Administration. In March of 1961 Mr. Moscoso was appointed Ambassador to Venezuela. Eight months later the President called him back to become Assistant Administrator for Latin America of the Agency for International Development and United States Coordinator of the Alliance for Progress.

DEAN RUSK was born in Cherokee County, Georgia. He started his international and academic career as a Rhodes Scholar at Oxford University, and later was Associate Professor of Government and Dean of the Faculty at Mills College, California. After World War II, during which he took part in two campaigns in the Burma theatre, Mr. Rusk served in both the State and War Departments. In 1949 he became the first Assistant Secretary of State for United Nations Affairs, subsequently being appointed Deputy Under-Secretary of State and Assistant Secretary for Far Eastern Affairs. In 1952 Mr. Rusk was named President of the Rockefeller Foundation, a position he left to become Secretary of State in January, 1961.

JOHN C. DREIER is Visiting Professor of Latin American Affairs and Director of the Inter-American Center at the School of Advanced International Studies, The Johns Hopkins University. Prior to his present appointment in 1961, Mr. Dreier was, for almost twenty years, associated with the Bureau of Inter-American Affairs of the State Department and from 1951 to 1960 served as United States Representative and Ambassador on the Council of the Organization of American States and the Inter-American Peace Committee. He has traveled widely in Latin America and has represented the United States at numerous international conferences.

INTRODUCTION

John C. Dreier

ADOPTION BY the United States of the policy towards Latin America which has been embodied in the Alliance for Progress marked a change in the nature and scope of this country's relations with the other American republics that has been only gradually recognized and even more slowly understood. The launching of the Alliance by President Kennedy in March, 1961, and its adoption as an inter-American program at the OAS Conference at Punta del Este, Uruguay, the following August, were actions widely hailed throughout both North and South America. Only recently, however, have the people of the hemisphere begun to sense the deeper implications of the change in policy and attitude that is involved—a change of tidal character that may best be likened to that which, about thirty years ago, marked the transition from the United States' policy of intervention in Latin America to the policy of the Good Neighbor.

Like most deep changes in human affairs, the evolution of the Alliance for Progress is the result of different motivations, and draws upon varied sources of inspiration and effort. It was baptized and given its dramatic send-off by President Kennedy in his speech of March 13, 1961, and in his special message to Congress on the following day. But important debates, proposals, decisions, and actions that had taken place over a period of several years, both in the United States and Latin America, contributed to laying the groundwork for the Alliance. The chapters that follow relate some of the steps through which United States policy evolved in the direction of the Alliance. They describe, also, some of the ideas that have emanated from Latin American thinkers in recent years and demands from the countries of that area for policies and actions—both in the domestic and international fields—that have now been embodied in the purposes of the Alliance for Progress.

This joint responsibility emphasizes the fact that the Alliance must be understood in the light of the whole history of hemisphere relations which has been marked by the increased sharing of responsibility among the republics of North and South America for the achievement of their peace and security, their political liberties, and their economic and social progress. During the period from the mid-1930's to the mid-1950's the Good Neighbor Policy made possible the creation of an effective multilateral system for the protection of the sovereignty and independence of the American states, replacing the unilateral, interventionist exercise of this function by the United States. We may envisage the new policy of the Alliance for Progress as the basis for the creation of a greatly needed, co-operative system for the achievement of the political, economic, and social progress, which is the outstanding goal of the Latin American peoples in our times. The Alliance for Progress is, as much as anything, a matter of a new attitude: a willingness on the part of both the United States and Latin America to recognize broader common goals and to devote new resources and joint efforts to their fulfillment in the coming decade.

The Alliance for Progress is not, therefore, so much a precise term to cover a specific set of undertakings or commitments as it is a broadly-conceived set of objectives and methods. The Charter of Punta del Este, in which the Alliance was set forth as an inter-American program, reveals its full scope.[1] Its cen-

[1] See appendix for text.

INTRODUCTION   xv

tral purpose is to increase the rate of economic growth in the Latin American countries in order to raise the living standards of their people. An annual growth rate of 2.5 per cent per capita is established as the minimum target for every country. To accomplish this, a series of economic measures are recognized as indispensable: the diversification of economies by promoting investment and industrialization; the improvement of agricultural production; the stabilization of commodity markets; the stimulation of Latin American economic integration and common markets; and the maintenance of stable price levels.

Economic development, however, is also understood to be impossible without concurrent improvement in social conditions. A more equitable distribution of the national income lies at the heart of this phase of the Alliance. Moreover, industrialized societies require an educated and trained working force, from top engineers and scientists to skilled laborers. Public health and adequate housing become more urgent in concentrated metropolitan population centers. These desirable benefits of economic development cannot, under modern conditions of public psychology, wait until after a new, productive industrial system has been set in motion. Their urgency was stressed at Punta del Este, and specific goals were also set for some of these social programs: for example, the elimination of adult illiteracy and the assurance of at least six years of primary schooling for every child throughout the region within the ten-year period.

Achievement of these goals, under the most favorable circumstances, would represent a long, difficult, and ambitious undertaking. It is the more so in the face of certain obstacles that are unfortunately so prominent in the Latin American scene today. The population explosion in the area is proceeding at a more rapid rate than anywhere else in the world. The Latin American countries thus face a large task in even preventing per-capita economic growth rates from falling behind, let alone assuring their increase. The unfavorable trend during recent years of the prices received by the Latin American countries for their basic commodity exports adds another major obstacle to ambitious development programs. Receipts of foreign exchange have declined just as the demands for it increase under the requirements of industrialization programs.

Finally, the Charter of Punta del Este recognizes that no program of economic development in Latin America can succeed in achieving that measure of social justice which is the basic goal of the peoples of this hemisphere, as elsewhere, without drastic changes in the economic and social institutions of the Latin American countries. Reform of the centuries-old systems of land tenure is seen as essential to create better rural living conditions, check the excessive migration of rural workers to the overcrowded cities, and permit the introduction of more efficient methods of land use. Modernization of tax policies and collection procedures is stressed as a necessary step toward better mobilization of the large amounts of domestic capital that must be applied to desirable economic and social purposes. For these and other internal reforms, the Latin American countries themselves must provide the necessary initiative, determination, and political action. In the Charter of Punta del Este, ratifying the earlier Act of Bogotá, they have acknowledged this responsibility, and the United States has pledged its support for their efforts.

Lack of understanding of the immensity of the problems involved in striving towards the great goals of the Alliance has led to dangerous impatience on both sides. One cause of confusion has been the tendency to think of the Alliance in terms of a "Marshall Plan" for Latin America—a misconception held not only by those Latin Americans who were primarily impressed with the large sums of U.S. investment in postwar Europe but also by some people in this country who fail to perceive fundamental differences between the two situations. The Marshall Plan made possible the restoration of an already advanced industrial system, where attitudes, techniques, and other aspects of compe-

INTRODUCTION

tence were freely available, and the capacity to modernize and take advantage of large scale help was great. The European countries knew what had to be done and how to do it. The Alliance for Progress faces a situation in which few countries are approaching even the "take-off" stage in economic development; in which the lack of educated and technically trained people is enormous; in which experience with an industrial society and its social and political problems is limited; and in which serious obstacles of a social and economic and political nature stand in the way of the development of that kind of modern society envisioned in the Act of Bogotá and the Punta del Este declarations.

Patience and understanding are, therefore, along with determination, prime requisites in the prosecution of the Alliance for Progress. Understanding is needed, moreover, not only of the profound and difficult nature of the problems to be overcome. It is needed also with regard to the *way* in which those problems will be met. The authorities who have contributed the chapters of this book stress more than once the folly of expecting a Yankee blue-print to be adopted in the modernization of Latin American societies. What will be done in those countries will be done in Latin American ways; the emphasis must be upon the fundamental goals rather than upon specific or detailed methods for reaching them. What was good, or even possible, for a growing economic giant in the nineteenth and early twentieth centuries will not necessarily prove adequate or suitable for the group of twenty very different Latin American nations in which the process of modernization must be telescoped into a few decades. Economic concepts must be re-examined with open minds. Political crises are inevitable under the stress of social pressure, and Latin American response thereto will not always be according to North American procedures. But we may take confidence in the fact that the Latin American people are evidencing an increasing determination to create and maintain free political institutions and to protect themselves from the current form of imperialist enslavement that is being purveyed by Moscow and Peiping and their accomplices in Havana.

The five lectures included in this volume touch upon most of these factors and many others. They do not, however, by any means exhaust the vast field of the Alliance for Progress and its manifold impact upon the lives of the 400 million people who make up the twenty-one American republics. The problem of population growth, for example, is one which calls for considerably more attention than has been possible here. Another area in which a great deal of creative thought is necessary is the means of strengthening progressive, democratic political parties and other similarly oriented instrumentalities for mobilizing public opinion, in order to assure adequate support for carrying out the aims of the Alliance. The agenda of topics for future consideration can easily be extended.

The following chapters should be viewed only as first steps in opening the doors of wider public comprehension of what is involved in this most challenging undertaking in the history of the inter-American system. It is hoped these essays will thus contribute to the development of that enlightened public opinion and support which are essential to the success of the new Alliance.

THE ALLIANCE FOR PROGRESS:
PROBLEMS AND PERSPECTIVES

1

THE ALLIANCE FOR PROGRESS: HISTORIC ROOTS

Milton S. Eisenhower

THE AMERICAN PEOPLES, imbued with cardinal concepts of human dignity, mutuality in human relations and consecrated intelligence, ask nothing more of the world society than that it respect their determination to be free and independent, ever striving for justice and rising levels of well-being for all.

It is a shocking anachronism that, at the very time the American nations are working for social reforms which would discard historic social stratifications inimical to human dignity, an extra-continental conspiratorial force should seek to engulf us with age-old fetters of the omniscient state and omnipotent fate.

Understanding Inter-American Relations

This coincidence of exalted and degraded efforts yields the misleading impression that the Alliance for Progress, formulated in the Act of Bogotá and finalized and proclaimed in the Charter of Punta del Este, is merely a negative response of free men to the threat of communist totalitarianism. This view is accepted by the uncritical press and by uninformed citizens. It is imperative, I think, to set the record straight. That is why I am happy that the School of Advanced International Studies of The Johns Hopkins University has sponsored this series of lectures which, I trust, will contribute to deeper understanding of the origins, positive purposes and potentialities of the Alliance. Genuine understanding is essential to its success.

This was recognized by the representatives of the American nations who formulated the Act of Bogotá, in 1960, and the Charter of Punta del Este, in 1961. I confess I have derived satisfaction from the conference declarations in this regard, for I have long insisted that the greatest impediment to fruitful co-operation among the American republics is lack of mutual understanding, not only with respect to acute problems requiring resolution but also with respect to one another's attitudes and aims. I have repeatedly recommended the creation in each of the American republics of commissions of influential citizens who would accept responsibility for seeing to it that harmful misconceptions are replaced with truth regarding inter-American relations. I hope the urge we share in having the Alliance for Progress attain its goals will cause us to build institutions dedicated to better understanding of one another.

Present efforts to construct a better life in freedom in this hemisphere are natural and inevitable forward steps in a long evolutionary process which would have reached this point of decision even had an egocentric Cuban leader not betrayed his people by delivering his nation to the iron control of the international communist conspiracy. Certainly I see the Alliance as a positive program of enlightened peoples to achieve, at last, that justice for all which is sanctified in our cherished religious convictions. Admittedly the threat of Castro-communism hastened decisions and actions. It did not cause or create them.

My analysis of the historic roots of the Alliance for Progress must be frankly that of a United States citizen, for my own deep concern and studies have always focused on means of strengthening United States policies and programs as they affect Latin America.

In glancing back into history from this age of mass communication and enlightenment, we see much that appalls us. Those who lived history, sensitive to the moods and forces of their time, may have felt that they were acting honorably. But attitudes have changed. Hence every nation today has cause to be ashamed of some things in its past. Slavery, crusades and inquisitions in the mission of religion, imperialism, fratricidal struggles for power—these were once the measure of all men.

But I believe the record of the United States in its dealings with our neighboring republics—with all its blemishes—ranks high in any comparative study of the lives of nations.

We began with a protective attitude which, unfortunately, evolved into patronizing imperialism. Imperialism was, in time, displaced by legal recognition of the juridical equality of states. Exploitation yielded to mutual helpfulness. And even the concept of nonintervention eventually gave way to a hemispheric policy of collective insistence that social justice be achieved for the masses of Latin American peoples.

Early Attitudes

We may view the history of inter-American relations as dividing into four major periods.

The first began with the wars of independence and extended essentially to the opening of the twentieth century. It was a period marked by a condescending but protective attitude in the United States and varying degrees of Yankee phobia in Latin America.

When the Spanish and Portuguese colonies gained independence, the United States was the first to extend recognition to them. Then, when President Monroe warned European nations to stay out of the Western Hemisphere, Latin American leaders were exultant. The relative good will of the nineteenth century was marred on several occasions, especially by United States expansion at the expense of Mexico—an expansion which was viewed as a threat to Latin American security generally and as an affront to its peoples. The fantastic adventures of William Walker, a Yankee who established himself as dictator of Nicaragua, and constant talk of the possibility of our annexing Cuba also contributed to Latin American distrust. But this feeling diminished as the new nations stabilized themselves, as prideful nationalism flourished, as cultural intercourse increased, and as the United States indirectly helped Mexico free itself from French domination. Coincidentally, mushrooming French and British investments in Latin America engendered misgivings about Europeans, leading even to an intellectual reaction against European customs, which were blamed by such men as Domingo Sarmiento, of Argentina, and José de Victorino de Lastarria, of Chile, for the lack of progress in Latin America.

As the century neared its end, good will among the American nations was sufficient to permit the holding of an inter-American conference which sought unsuccessfully to establish a system of arbitration in settling Latin American boundary disputes and thus of eliminating the danger of European intervention. This was the apogee of inter-American relations between the 1820's and the 1930's.

The Period of Intervention

Complicating factors—as the twentieth century opened—ushered in a second period of relationships, highlighted by our intervening repeatedly in Latin American affairs—a fact which, I shall

HISTORIC ROOTS

indicate, retarded the development of programs for social justice now envisaged in the Alliance for Progress.

Expansionism was the driving force of nations at the close of the nineteenth century. European powers were engaged in imperialistic pursuits in Africa, the Middle East, and Asia. Extension of this influence into the Western Hemisphere was feared by the United States, which was emerging as a world power in its own right. A profound psychological change occurred. Fostered by political leaders and industrialists, and encouraged by citizens who were charmed by a new sense of power, the United States abandoned a portion of its isolationist policy which had been adhered to since the days of Washington. The nation succumbed to imperialism. Eyes turned southward toward the strategic Caribbean.

The brief struggle to help free Cuba was the response of decent people against the brutal excesses of Spain, but also evident was our swaddling ambition for expansion. The imposition of the Platt Amendment and the proclamation of the Roosevelt Corollary to the Monroe Doctrine—which rationalized our right to intervene in hemispheric affairs—revealed the degree to which the United States was infected with the global disease of imperialism. Blatant assertions of the hegemonic rights of the United States stirred Latin Americans to a fever of anti-Yankeeism.

If in its long intervention in Cuba the United States had fostered the degree of social justice which it cherished for its own people, the whole course of United States–Latin American relations would have been far different. The hemisphere need not have been blighted by a Batista or a Castro. A priceless opportunity was missed.

Intervention in Cuba was followed by penetrations into the internal affairs of Colombia, Panamá, Nicaragua, Haiti, the Dominican Republic, Mexico, and other countries. Some of these interventions, especially during the Wilsonian period, were undertaken in the pious belief that democratic institutions could be imposed—that temporary intervention was justified by the ultimate aim of establishing democratic norms. But such a result was not obtained; the self-serving idealism was scorned by Latin Americans, who were enraged by the blue-coated marines and sailors on Spanish-American soil. In this period the United States altered the traditional policy of diplomatic recognition: discarded was the concept that recognition meant only that a government could maintain internal order and would abide by international commitments. Substituted was a policy of withholding recognition until regimes had been legalized by elective processes. This was another fruitless form of intervention.

Economic issues began to inflame the prevailing ill will. Tariff acts of the 1920's and early 1930's were designed solely to protect United States producers. Concurrently, United States private investment in Latin America attained substantial proportions. Charges arose that many United States companies were exploitive—showing little concern for local development and welfare—and that our tariff acts were designed to keep Latin America in a colonial status, a mere supplier of cheap raw commodities.

The unhappy aspects of this era lessened as the United States restored the traditional policy of recognizing foreign governments, began withdrawing its forces from several countries, initiated a more enlightened diplomacy as epitomized in Mexico by Ambassador Dwight Morrow, abrogated the Roosevelt Corollary to the Monroe Doctrine and sent its President-elect on the first Presidential mission of good will to the nations of Latin America.

The Good Neighbor

But it was, of course, the promulgation of the Good Neighbor Policy which ushered in the third period of inter-American relations. By treaties, interventionism was discarded. Accepted was the policy of mutual respect, juridical equality of States, and settlement of disputes by negotiation. Offensive economic protectionism was replaced by a program of mutually beneficial tariff adjustments.

The concept of reciprocity was dramatized by the peaceful settlement of a major difficulty between the United States and Mexico. We limited ourselves to making diplomatic representations, merely insisting that just repayment should be made for North American oil holdings expropriated earlier by Mexico. We accepted expropriation as Mexico's legal right, never considered the use of force, and agreed to Mexico's proposal for the method by which repayment could be determined by equal powers—a feat which would have been impossible twenty years before.

The Good Neighbor Policy earned applause in Latin America. United States business enterprises, finding they had to act on their own to prevent discriminatory treatment, discarded exploitive practices, worked for the benefit of host countries, paid taxes, raised wages, and often built schools, highways, and hospitals. On the whole, United States enterprisers became business statesmen.

So genuine did good feeling become that during World War II most nations of Latin America co-operated wholeheartedly in contributing to the defeat of Naziism. The Act of Chapultepec, the Rio Treaty of Reciprocal Assistance, and the Charter of the Organization of American States provided monumental evidence that the American republics had become equal partners in law, in spirit, and in a mutual determination to protect national independence and freedom.

Economic Issues Become Paramount

Unfortunately, this happy condition became clouded as a fourth period of inter-American relations began in the late 1940's. Economic issues became paramount.

During World War II, increased sales to the United States had enabled many of the nations of Latin America to accumulate large dollar reserves. As purchases from us became possible, prices of needed goods reached higher levels. War price controls in the United States had held down the cost of commodities purchased, whereas postwar sales were at free-market levels. Therefore, intense dissatisfaction developed over the fact that primary commodities sold by Latin American nations were subject to wide price fluctuations, sometimes as much as 50 per cent in one year, whereas the prices of processed goods bought by Latin America continued to increase. In anger, many Latin Americans unwarrantedly charged that the United States fixed prices to the detriment of its neighbors.

Leaders in Latin America realized that they would have to diminish their dependence on primary commodities. They determined to accelerate the development of indigenous industries, to expand, diversify, and increase the efficiency of agriculture, and to enhance the efficiency of the human resource through better education, health facilities, and low-cost housing.

As this demand grew, the United States seemingly became preoccupied with the reconstruction of war-devastated Europe and, later, with the creation of a global defense posture that would prevent a new savagery from engulfing free men.

Many Latin Americans did not recognize the free-world dimensions and values of the Marshall Plan and mutual security programs. They viewed these efforts as competitors for the largess of the United States. Actually, the generous outpouring of United States resources to rebuild a ravaged Europe was of great benefit to Latin America, for Europe was restored as a vital economic unit and thus became again a large purchaser of Latin American exports. The construction of a defense perimeter around the imperialist communist powers was for the protection of all free nations, including Latin America.

But, impatient for economic growth that required immense quantities of foreign capital, Latin America tended to ignore

HISTORIC ROOTS

these benefits. In anger and injured pride, Latin Americans charged that the failure of the United States to extend to them the benefits of these gigantic world efforts proved that we considered other areas more important to our future. Thus convinced, they became openly critical of the fact that they were not consulted in the early stages of the development of the United Nations and that consultations with them on the formation of NATO, for example, were purely perfunctory. Gone, they felt, was the Good Neighbor Policy with its rich promise of partnership. This view, of course, held highly unfortunate misconceptions.

United States aid to Latin America began in a small way in 1938 when the Export-Import Bank committed loans of some $200,000,000 to Latin American governments in a two-year period. Technical assistance started in 1942. The Lend-Lease program sent a quarter of a billion dollars to Latin America. In the 1940's, Latin American trade with the United States increased several-fold and was sustained at the higher level. More generous trade rules were developed.

The decade of the fifties witnessed a tremendous increase in United States assistance to Latin America. Technical assistance was expanded—to attack problems of education, agriculture, health, and business management. Large quantities of food were shipped to meet emergencies. The net flow of public and private United States capital to Latin America more than doubled, reaching $1.7 billion in one year. By 1958, United States loans and investments in Latin America totaled $11 billion. The capital of several public lending institutions was increased to the point that lending capacity exceeded demand. A new national credit agency was brought into being for the purpose of making loans repayable in local currencies, and two new international credit instruments were created on the initiative of the United States.

At the same time, the United States, discarding historic attitudes and policies, vigorously supported the development of common markets in Latin America in the belief that wider market potentials would speed economic development and increase the credit worthiness of the participating nations. Whereas for years the United States had remained coldly aloof from primary commodity problems, our government now initiated the creation of cotton, lead, zinc, coffee, and other commodity study groups; sanctioned a coffee stabilization plan; and committed the United States to helping find feasible methods of alleviating the critical problem of fluctuating price relationships.

But this increased tempo of effort to foster economic growth was accompanied by a rising tide of criticism in Latin America. The criticism came not from government officials but from leaders of private groups and intellectuals. A new problem, smoldering for years, had suddenly burst into the consciousness of the peoples of the Americas. This new element was indigenously Latin American, but in the general public mind and propaganda the United States was identified with it and to a considerable extent blamed for it.

It was the element of inequality—of lack of social justice for the masses in some of the countries.

The average per capita income in one nation was $75 a year, about $800 in another. Disparities within some of the countries were even greater. In them, a few families might be fabulously wealthy; they might own a substantial portion of the productive resources. In such a country the middle income families were few; the masses were desperately poor—an ocean of uneducated, impoverished, neglected humanity.

Economic and social stratification had been evident from the beginning of Latin American history. Suddenly, modern communication had alerted the masses to the fact that poverty and degradation were neither universal nor inevitable. There arose insistent demands for reform—reform which would enable productive enterprise to benefit *all* the people.

The rising tide of discontent with the prevailing order shaped attitudes toward the United States. It was argued that our private and public capital in Latin America strengthened oppressive systems and mores which perpetuated the very injustices the people had come to detest.

The United States faced a serious dilemma: the extension of additional credit, no matter how voluminous, would intensify the growing dislike of the United States. But if we were to insist that, as a condition of obtaining loans, recipient governments would have to change tax, land, labor, and other laws, as desired by the discontented, and as needed to achieve social justice, we would be charged with intervening once again in the internal affairs of Latin America.

Leaders in the United States were still sensitive to the waves of criticism that had engulfed us during the era of our interventionism. We therefore adhered to the concept that internal change was the exclusive responsibility of individual countries—that we had no choice but to work with established governments and institutions, regardless of the degree of social justice achieved or envisaged.

This dilemma was formidable and seemed impervious to a happy solution.

Towards a New Economic Policy

The first significant step toward a possible solution was taken when the United States cast aside its opposition to the creation of an inter-American development bank. For many years the United States had insisted that existing international and national credit institutions could supply all credit needed in Latin America for sound development—that an additional institution would cause confusion and higher administrative costs without swelling the outflow of funds. But the times called for new thinking. An inter-American development institution, governed by the participating nations, with authority to make both hard and soft loans, held several promises. First, decisions on loan applications would be made co-operatively; thus there would be no justification for identifying the United States with project developments that might, while improving the economies, continue to strengthen the prevailing order. Second, if conditions were attached to loans, in the hope of spreading more widely the benefits of economic growth, the intervention involved or implied would have been collectively determined. In other words, an agency of the Americas might help to solve the dilemma: desirable social changes might be fostered through credit, while avoiding the malodorous charges that had arisen as the United States sought sincerely but unilaterally to promote economic development in Latin America.

It should be noted that the vital changes in attitudes and policies which I have mentioned—with respect to common markets, commodity stabilization, greatly increased aid, and a new inter-American bank—occurred before Castro took power in Cuba.

In February, 1959, a month after Castro's assumption of power, when he was still applauded by majorities in the United States and throughout the hemisphere, the United States presented to the Committee of Twenty-One of the OAS suggestions which foreshadowed provisions of the Act of Bogotá. The proposal envisaged not only an increased flow of credit but also better development planning, increased trade, intensified efforts to promote common markets, stabilization to the extent feasible of primary commodity markets, and the beginning of social change through the financing of low-cost housing.

On April 20, 1960, the Secretary of State, in an address in the Pan American Union, intimated that further changes in policy were soon to come. Said he: "If we support the premise that the dignity of the individual in a free society is strengthened when he acquires his own home, so must we also recognize the importance of land ownership to the man who works the land. . . . Land distribution is a problem of the hemisphere, demanding

HISTORIC ROOTS

the attention of all nations and the Organization of American States."

Several months later, the President of the United States sent to Congress an urgent recommendation. We must, he said, "help our Latin neighbors accelerate their efforts to strengthen the social and economic structure of their nations and to improve the status of their individual citizens." He requested enactment of authorizing legislation prior to the meeting of the Committee of Twenty-One which was to convene at Bogotá on September 5, less than a month later.

On August 15, 1960, the Under-Secretary of State, testifying before the Senate Foreign Relations Committee, said: "While there has been a steady rise in . . . national incomes throughout [Latin America], millions of under-privileged have not benefited. . . . The distribution of national incomes in many countries has been far from equitable, with the bulk of the income going to a very small portion of the population. . . . In some countries, progress has been impeded by outdated economic, legal and social institutions. . . . The result is . . . to deny a large part of the population an opportunity to share equitably the growth of the national product."

Existing agencies would continue to extend credit to Latin American countries, he explained. What was needed was new authority to initiate programs for social improvement.

He spoke eloquently of the substandard living conditions of the rural peoples of Latin America who constitute more than fifty per cent of the population. Land-tenure and land-taxation systems, dating from colonial times, had led to demand for land reform. Further, a lack of social development was reflected in inadequate education, poor health, and social unrest in the cities. It was a vicious cycle, for lack of education and poor health were major causes of social backwardness. The cycle had to be broken.

So intense had social unrest become, he said, that free democratic institutions were threatened throughout the hemisphere. What was needed was an immediate assault on social problems by the nations of the hemisphere, all working together, each carrying its share of the burden. An initial authorization of a half-billion dollars, later to be augmented, was requested; most of this fund would be spent through the new Inter-American Development Bank.

The Congress acted swiftly. On September 8, 1960, Public Law 735—an act to stimulate social development in Latin America—was on the statute books.

Two days before the Congress completed its work on the Act, representatives of the American republics were in Bogotá. The Under-Secretary of State, speaking for the United States said: "By our decision we can, if we will, launch a far-reaching attack on the poverty, ignorance, and lack of social justice which, even in this 20th Century world, still oppress so many of our fellow citizens in Latin America."

The fundamental task was to outline the route by which the people of the Americas could achieve the material progress they desired without sacrifice of human rights and freedoms. Powerful impetus should be given to constructive forces of domestic action and international co-operation, working hand in hand, for the greatest task of our time was to raise the living standards of the masses. The inter-American bank should become an effective, multilateral instrument in providing essential planning and financing. The United States was willing to do its full share. The Under-Secretary suggested a ten-year massive effort.

On September 12, 1960, the American republics, Cuba dissenting, proclaimed the Act of Bogotá. Since by then United States Public Law 735 was in effect, it was known that help for social improvement would be available. Hence the significance of the Act of Bogotá was agreement by the Latin American nations themselves to act together in solving social and economic problems. They pledged that the aspiration of their peoples for improved status and better life would be met; that they would give highest priority to meeting social needs, through reforms in taxation, land distribution, education, health, and housing.

The act outlined measures to be taken. If the measures are carried out faithfully, the whole human society of our neighbors will begin a process of far-reaching alteration. This will mean, in turn, that the aid we extend—public and private, orthodox and unorthodox, unilateral and multilateral—should, if men have not become wholly cynical, create that friendly co-operative community of free peoples which we of this country fervently desire.

Launching the Alliance

Six months after Bogotá, the President of the United States, speaking in the White House to representatives of the Latin American nations, promised anew that the United States would co-operate in a vast effort "to satisfy the basic needs of the American people for homes, work and land, health, and schools."

For the first time, a Chief Executive of the United States candidly said, as the Under-Secretary of State had done at Bogotá, that our aid would be of limited value unless they themselves vigorously fostered programs of social reform and used the proffered external funds in support of such programs.

Such a statement by a United States President in the period immediately following our forays into interventionism would surely have met with extreme hostility. But now there was such shared concern with the basic problem of Latin America that the President's meaningful phrase, Alliance for Progress, was greeted with spontaneous applause.

"Throughout Latin America," he said, "millions of men and women suffer the daily degradations of hunger and poverty. . . . They lack decent shelter or protection from disease. . . . Each day the problem grows more urgent." Unless the great mass of Americans shared in increasing prosperity, he said "our Alliance, our revolution and our dream will have failed."

The President emphasized the concept of co-operation and self-help. "If this effort is made," he said, "then outside assistance will give a vital impetus to progress—without it, no amount of help will advance the welfare of the people."

In August, 1961, ministerial representatives of the American republics met at Punta del Este to formulate operational details of the Alliance. The objectives of Bogotá were translated into specific targets. Thus, for example, the goal of economic advance enunciated at Bogotá became at Punta del Este a specific target of five per cent increase each year in gross national product of the Latin American countries.

Every citizen of North, Central, and South America should be knowledgable about the decisions recorded at Punta del Este. One document in particular, a Declaration to the Peoples of America, may find a place of dignity and significance comparable to that of the constitutions of the American nations. A few excerpts from the Declaration indicate its flavor:

> Inspired by the principles consecrated in the Charter of the Organization of American States . . . and in the Act of Bogotá, the representatives of the American republics hereby agree to establish an Alliance for Progress: a vast effort to bring a better life to all the peoples of the Continent.
>
> This Alliance is established on the basic principle that free men working through institutions of representative democracy can best satisfy man's aspirations. . . .

They set these goals:

> To accelerate economic and social development. . . . To provide decent homes for all our people. . . . To encourage comprehensive agrarian reform [so that] the land will become for the man who works it the basis of his economic stability. . . .
>
> To wipe out illiteracy. . . .

To press forward with programs of health and sanitation. . . .

To reform tax laws, to punish tax evasion . . . , to redistribute the national income. . . .

To maintain monetary and fiscal policies which, while avoiding . . . inflation, will protect the purchasing power of the many . . . and form an adequate basis for economic development.

To stimulate private enterprise. . . .

To find a lasting solution to the grave problem caused by excessive price fluctuations. . . .

The American nations pledged that they would devote at least $100 billion in ten years toward achieving these goals. The United States indicated that 20 per cent of this sum could reasonably be expected to come from external sources, principally in public funds.

And so was reached a climax in a long evolutionary process. An unprecedented hemispheric effort had been launched. We were embarked on a mission of social change for justice and rising levels of living.

The Political Challenge

I may, I think, without impinging upon subsequent chapters in this volume, ask a pertinent question: Can the United States be depended upon to adhere to and help finance the Alliance during the coming decade?

It is noteworthy that the relevant United States attitudes, policies, and commitments have involved two national administrations of different political parties. We may therefore be confident that the Alliance has the support of most of our people and of our elected representatives. Further, since these bi-partisan commitments were given when the United States was suffering serious imbalances in international payments, we may say with assurance that in solving our international financial problems we shall not decrease our support of this ten-year program.

I am convinced that the only development which could lessen the zeal of the people of the United States for the Alliance would be a failure of the Latin American nations themselves either to carry out the social reforms and economic developments envisaged at Bogotá and Punta del Este or to uphold the democratic concepts enunciated there.

Many friends of Latin America were disturbed when at Punta del Este in 1962 several nations found it inappropriate or inexpedient to go beyond the condemnation of Castro-communism and exclude the Cuban government from participation in the Organization of American States.

Harsh words were spoken in this country about this apparent departure from the spirit of the Alliance for Progress, for the Alliance places full faith in democratic institutions and in the ability of free people to establish social justice by peaceful means.

Castro-communism violates every precept of the Alliance. Castro's inhumanity is that of Trujillo, Pérez Jiménez, and Perón. His communism, however, is a threat to freedom in all the nations of the hemisphere. So good friends ask, "Do not our neighbors understand this?"

To find comprehension, we must again look back a few years. In the tumultuous months following Castro's victory, four issues emerged. First, was Cuba at last to enjoy democratic freedom, or simply to suffer another tyranny? Second, if tyranny were the unhappy result, would it be indigenous or would it—in defiance of policies to which the whole American community adheres—be dominated by a subversive extracontinental power? Third, would threatened expropriations be handled in harmony with international custom or would they be outright thefts? And fourth, would Castro, either as democratic leader or dictator, proceed with promised social reforms which initially had gained him the support of Cubans and of the hemisphere generally? As events unfolded, most persons in the United States, while not indifferent to the fourth of these issues, nonetheless gave primary attention to the first three. Most peoples in Latin America were more concerned with the fourth, the promise of social reform. Hence, the United States' attitude became deeply antagonistic; that in Latin America became ambivalent, though mainly sympathetic.

This initial divergence in attitude was due to a sharp change in *our* thinking, not in *theirs*. At the height of the revolutionary struggle and for a time after Castro seized power, he was applauded by most persons in the United States, as he was in Latin America. This was a natural reaction of most people who were disgusted with the brutality of Batista and deluded by Castro's repeated promises that, when the revolutionary forces succeeded, the constitution of 1940 would become the supreme law of the land. He guaranteed freedom of information, all rights set forth in the constitution, and general elections within a year after the defeat of Batista. His propaganda called for "a free and democratic Cuba dedicated to social and economic justice."

But shortly after he came to power, Castro began to reveal his true colors. His opponents were banished, jailed, or shot. Freedom of the press vanished. He seized, without compensation, a billion dollars in United States assets, which so frightened United States investors that the outflow of private capital to Latin America, totalling $600 million in 1958, sharply declined. Since then, repatriated capital has at times exceeded outflow.

Castro-communism became evident. The Communist party, which had supported Batista and dismissed Castro as of no importance, became the sole political party of Cuba. Communists took charge of the armed forces, economic and social planning, trade unions, university faculties, professional groups, and civic and farm organizations.

This betrayal of the announced goals of the revolution shocked the people of the United States. We broke relations and suspended nearly all trade with Cuba.

In Latin America, the great sea of underprivileged, with no vested interest in the established orders of their own countries, continued to praise the Cuban revolution. They believed they were witnessing a repetition of the Mexican revolution. It, too, had had its years of extremism, but eventually smoothed out into a program of continuing economic development with justice for all classes. The masses of Latin America concluded, at least for a time, that extremism was an inescapable phase of any movement to change a historic system that yielded them in their own countries nothing but hopelessness. They overlooked the fact that leaders of the Mexican revolution sincerely sought to create a democratic society. Expropriations of property were accompanied by compensation. There was never a hint of the imposition of an extracontinental authority on Mexico; indeed, no country is more wedded to the concept of independence and non-intervention.

Fortunately, most Latin American presidents, cabinet ministers, and other knowledgeable leaders soon saw Castro-communism for what it is. Many who at first were sympathetic became disenchanted, and their countries withdrew recognition from the Castro regime. At San José, in August 1960, they joined in condemning foreign intervention in the affairs of the hemisphere. But some leaders at Punta del Este in 1962 hesitated to take collective action against Castro. Several knew that in their countries there existed the grave danger of uprisings by the oppressed. Action against Castro might spark such uprisings. Violence in those countries could result in communist dictatorships. This would be catastrophic for them and for us.

As Castro-communism fanatically tries to spread its influence to other Latin American countries, it receives organized support.

In Latin America are 200,000 dedicated communists with about $100 million a year at their disposal for adroit efforts to

HISTORIC ROOTS

promote violence and discord. They are organized on the Leninist principle that only the most trustworthy may be members of the party. Others may be their fellow-travellers. Fortunately, communists and their followers constitute a small minority—but it is a sly and disproportionately influential minority.

The communists and fellow-travellers are bitterly opposed to the Alliance for Progress. Through some three hundred of their own publications and on purchased radio time, they are attacking the Act of Bogotá and the Charter of Punta del Este with uninhibited violence. They do not want peaceful change. They want bloodshed, for in violence they believe they will have their greatest opportunity to seize power as they did in Cuba, where only 25,000 belonged to the party.

At the opposite extreme are the oligarchists who own vast empires of land, enjoy historic privilege, and often send their surplus wealth to the United States and Europe for investment rather than keeping it at home to speed development. Some of the oligarchists, like the communists, are opposed to the Alliance for Progress. They want no change. However, others of the elite realize that the stratifications of the fifteenth to nineteenth centuries cannot be sustained in the twentieth and that they must therefore foster democratic development or suffer as did the privileged of Cuba.

Between these extremes are the democratic groups—ranging from some of the privileged and most of the highly educated, through nearly all of the middle classes, to the desperately poor. Though they cover a broad political spectrum, they all want to preserve democratic institutions. They want nothing more extreme than the type of social justice we ourselves are fortunate enough to enjoy in our mature society.

The submerged masses, of course, have few spokesmen. They are not articulate. Often they have little organized power. Into this vacuum, university students have moved as a potent force.

In Santiago, a few months before the Act of Bogotá, I spoke with the President of the Chilean Student Federation, which has a membership of 25,000. He said that all of them are Christians, anti-communist, and pro-democratic.

He asked: "Has the United States become a satisfied nation, one which fights for the maintenance of the prevailing order in Latin America? This dangerous image is being accepted more every day. If this is true, we must respectfully say to you that the United States will have little or nothing to offer the younger generation and the immense multitude of the poor who compose 90 per cent of the Latin American population."

In the United States and Western Europe, he went on, it made sense to fight for the prevailing order, because social order represented values widely shared: personal freedom, social justice, equality before the law. But to defend the existing social order in Latin America meant only maintaining the privilege of a thin layer of the population which controlled the power and wealth.

The students were bitterly opposed to communism. "There are," he said, "impassable barriers separating us from communist ideology and methods, but no one should be deceived. . . . If Christianity and democracy fail in the coming ten or fifteen years in giving work and bread, dignity and security, to the poor, then the fiery breath of communism will cover the earth."

This moving statement by a university leader should not be passed by lightly. University students in Latin America may not speak for political leaders. They may often speak for submerged humanity.

My own assessment is that the democratic forces in Latin America *can* prevail. But they must move rapidly, and they must have our sustained help.

Hence, in my judgment, the failure of some nations at Punta del Este in 1962 to vote for the expulsion of Castro's Cuba from the Organization of American States should not deter us from putting the full weight of our faith behind the Alliance for Progress. Whatever may have caused hesitation on the part of six countries—fear of their own people, or legal niceties, or neutralism, or assumed bargaining power—we should remember that the Alliance was evolved largely without reference to Castro-communism, that the program would be imperative even if there were no communist threat, that it is wholly in harmony with our deepest religious and democratic convictions, and that our abiding purpose is positive, not negative. But the Alliance is, coincidentally, our best hope for smothering the evil that seeks to destroy the concept of associated free nations and to substitute an absolutism reminiscent of social man prior to the dawn of human freedom.

On both these bases, therefore, it is essential that at every turn we reaffirm our commitment to the inspiring concepts embodied in the Act Bogotá, the Charter of Punta del Este, and the Alliance for Progress. These constitute a modern Magna Carta of the Americas.

I have found some of my thoughts well stated in a recent *New York Times* editorial, which said: "The Alliance for Progress is more than the answer to the Cuban Revolution. It is an attempt to answer one of the most momentous and menacing problems of our times, which is how the economically underdeveloped areas of the world can meet the insistent popular demand for social justice and economic development. The Communist and, in theory, the Fascist systems offer a drastic method —revolution followed by totalitarian government. We say the goals can better be reached by our evolutionary, democratic, free system."

2

ECONOMIC ASPECTS OF THE ALLIANCE

Raúl Prebisch

CONVINCED OF THE NEED of clarifying the meaning of the Alliance for Progress, I will attempt to explain its economic significance from the Latin American point of view.[*]

But let me first recall that there are many in Latin America who for years have been advocating the need for profound changes in our economic and social structure to pave the way for an accelerated pace of economic and social development. It is no wonder, then, that for them the recognition accorded in the Charter of Punta del Este to the urgent need for these changes constitutes an event of far-reaching importance.

Indeed, the basic ideas underlying this document were conceived and gradually developed over a period of years in Latin America. For a long time we have constantly maintained the view that a vigorous movement of industrialization was imperative in the process of development. We have also reaffirmed the inevitability of land reform and other changes in the social struc-

---

[*] The present chapter is an expanded version of Dr. Prebisch's original paper, which the author kindly agreed to prepare in order to discuss some subjects more fully than was possible in the text made public at the time of the lecture.—Ed.

ture, in order to facilitate the massive adoption of modern technology and the progressive redistribution of the fruits of development. We called attention to the importance of the terms of trade, and the need to counteract their tendency to deteriorate through transformations in the economic structure; and we insistently advocated measures to attenuate their fluctuations. The idea of the Latin American Common Market emerged in our countries. And the need for a considerable enlargement of foreign funds to supplement a more intense mobilization of internal resources in order to accelerate the rhythm of development, was also preached for a long time from Latin America. Moreover, though facing strong opposition, we, the Latin Americans, were the ones who launched the idea of the need for systematic planning as the means to act in a conscious and deliberate way upon the economic and social forces and thus expedite the achievement of the great goals of development in an orderly and progressive fashion.

In times that are not yet far behind some of these ideas encountered very strong resistance, which was frequently couched in intractable and dogmatic terms. Now they are recognized as sound and valid and are largely embodied in the Charter of Punta del Este.

However, there has developed a rather peculiar tendency to present these ideas as having been conceived in the United States, or as constituting a ready-made American blueprint to be applied in Latin America. I am really concerned about this trend, for not only is it contrary to the facts, but its political implications are highly detrimental to the Alliance itself and to the broad popular support it requires in Latin America.

Latin America has to project its own image—its authentic image—in this process of development. We have to shape it according to our own ways of feeling and thinking and our own concepts of action. We cannot repeat or imitate the historical course of the capitalistic development of the most advanced countries. Consequently, we have to find our own path with our own creative powers. Naturally, this does not preclude intellectual influences from outside. On the contrary, we expect them; but these influences should be only an element—though a very important one—in the elaboration of our own system of thinking, helping to guide us in our efforts to act upon the economic and social process.

A year ago President Kennedy gave vigorous recognition to those Latin American ideas when he announced a new and bold policy of co-operation with respect to this region. It was a clear American response to an insistent Latin American challenge. He perceived the deep aspirations of the Latin American peoples for economic and social reform. Previously, President Roosevelt had also perceived strong Latin American feelings for independence and sovereignty, and for the first time in the history of our relations an American president was able to gather wide emotional support among the large masses of the Latin American population. But this is no longer sufficient. Now it is essential adequately to interpret and confront the deep-rooted and growing expectations of economic and social reform felt by our peoples.

Structural Obstacles to the Penetration of Modern Technology

The possibility of extirpating poverty and its inherent evils in Latin America as well as in the rest of the developing world is no longer a utopian idea. Indeed, the role of modern technology is to make it feasible. However, the rapid and balanced spread and assimilation of modern technology entail greater efforts that require, and must be accompanied by, those profound changes in the economic and social structure to which I referred earlier. Several structural obstacles are retarding or interfering with the orderly penetration of modern technology. I would like to clarify briefly the nature of these obstacles. Let us first start with the economic structure.

Industrialization and Import Substitution

Industrialization constitutes an outstanding expression of the changes needed in the Latin American economic structure. The reason for its need, although very clear and simple, has frequently been subject to misunderstandings within and without this region. Due to the evolution of production techniques as well as of consumer demand, when per-capita income increases persistently owing to the absorption of modern technology, the demand for industrial products grows at a much faster pace than the demand for primary products.

If this greater demand for manufactures could be fully met by imports from the industrial centers in exchange for foodstuffs and primary goods exported to them at satisfactory prices by Latin America, then this region's need to industrialize would not be so urgent. However, given the fact that the industrial centers also experience similar changes in the composition of the demand as per capita income increases, consumption and imports of Latin American primary goods grow very slowly. The protectionist policies followed by some industrialized countries in order to safeguard their own production, particularly in the agricultural sector, further restrict imports of Latin American origin.

Moreover, thanks to the constant advances in manufacturing techniques, the industrial centers—either through better utilization of traditional raw materials and their by-products or the replacement of these by synthetic materials—need and employ a decreasing proportion of imported raw materials for their industrial production. Consequently, Latin American industry must develop so as to satisfy the demand for manufactured goods that the region can no longer afford to import.

Industrialization and the Absorption of Manpower

This then is one of the important dynamic roles of industrialization. The other is the absorption of manpower released from the agricultural and other sectors of the economy as technical progress penetrates into them. Yet, even in those Latin American countries where the rate of industrial development has been rather high, the absorption of available manpower has been far from satisfactory. Large segments of the manpower force remain unemployed or underemployed, and this is one of the causes for persistent social tensions.

This phenomenon is caused by two main factors: first, the high rate of population increase; and second, the nature of modern technology. Let me explain this briefly. While we have a scarcity of capital and potentially abundant manpower, we are indiscriminately introducing production techniques conceived for and applied in advanced countries where the prevailing conditions are just the reverse. In the more advanced countries, technology is directed more and more towards economizing manpower; and this is the same technology which is available to countries in the course of development.

Labor-Saving and Labor-Absorbing Investments

This causes very serious dislocations in Latin America, since absorbing a rapidly expanding labor force means assimilating a technology which in fact tends to economize manpower. Thus, capital requirements greatly exceed the possibilities of capital accumulation in those countries.

The more productivity rises because of the saving in manpower resulting from the increase in investment per worker, the

ECONOMIC ASPECTS

more pressing becomes the need for capital accumulation, both in order to give productive employment to the manpower thus saved and to provide employment for the continuous stream of those entering into productive activity.

In other words, the progressive adoption of the technology of the large countries, because it economizes manpower, also necessitates a faster rate of economic growth. If this rate is low, the maladjustments resulting from shifts in the labor force will be greater. People will be shifted from occupations that are turning away workers before the occupations that can be expected to absorb manpower are in a position to do so. This leads to a congestion or a surplus of unemployed or underemployed manpower which, in addition to representing a waste of factors of production, may understandably lead to social tensions.

Capital accumulation must have a much higher growth rate than the labor force if labor-absorbing activities are to play a full part in providing productive employment for all the overflow of extra manpower from the activities that are turning labor away.

Balancing the Two Types of Investment

All this constitutes a problem that has not been properly clarified in Latin America; nor has due consideration been given to the tools needed to solve it. However, it is realized that no solution can be expected from the mere free play of private enterprise as was possible during the evolution of capitalism in the more advanced countries because capital accumulation went hand in hand with technological development. The entrepreneur tends to use forms of capital which increase his returns by economizing manpower, but the effect of this on the economy as a whole is not his concern.

Actually, to obviate these maladjustments deriving from shifts of the active population, what is needed is a suitable combination of capital investment leading to a saving in manpower, and the investment required to absorb both this manpower and its growth. The ratio between these two forms of investment is not arbitrary; it depends on the country's possibilities of development and the amount of capital available. However, there is a ratio of balance, and if investment that economizes in manpower exceeds its due proportion, the phenomenon of surplus manpower referred to above will occur.

The Dynamic Elements of the Population

A low level of capital accumulation and a slow growth rate produce not only stresses of the kind just described but equally, if not more, have important effects on social mobility and the emergence of dynamic elements of the population.

Each generation has its dynamic elements, which usually place their distinctive stamp upon it. There are individuals who are destined to play a decisive part in economics, technology, scientific and cultural matters, politics and trade unionism. In economics and technology, their task will be to organize and direct enterprises, initiate action, and assume risks and responsibilities. It is towards these persons that the drive for technological levelling-up, to which I shall refer later on, should be directed.

Such individuals constitute dynamic elements not only because of their special gifts but also because of their active role in promoting social mobility. A high rate of economic growth hastens this process, which in turn influences the growth rate. Hence the strategic importance of these dynamic elements. An annual growth of per-capita income of only one per cent, as is now the case, or of three per cent, not only determines whether the standard of living will be doubled within 70 years, or within less than 25. It also means something else of vital importance: the higher of these two rates will permit the rapid absorption into economic activity of these dynamic elements, broadening their horizons, whereas a moderate rate means the waste of a great part of these forces and mounting tensions which, if they fail to find an adequate outlet in economic activity, will eventually discover some way of bursting out of the economic and social bonds that contain them.

The Basic Flaws in Industrialization

This is not the only problem relating to industrialization in Latin America. Serious mistakes have affected its development due to improvisation and the pressure of group interests. In general, there has not been a rational industrialization policy in our countries.

The process of industrialization suffers from three main flaws, which have weakened its contribution to improving the standard of living. These are: first, all industrialization activity is directed towards the domestic market; second, the choice of industries to be established has been based more on circumstantial reasons than on considerations of economic yield; and last, industrialization has failed to overcome the external vulnerability of the Latin American countries.

The excessive channelling of industry toward the domestic market is a result of the development policy pursued in the Latin American countries and of the lack of international incentives to exports of industrial goods from the region.

Development policies have been discriminatory as regards exports. Assistance has been given—through tariffs or other restrictions—to industrial production for internal consumption but not to industrial production for export. The production of many industrial goods has thus been developed at a cost far above the international level, when they could have been obtained with a much smaller cost differential in exchange for exports of other industrial products which might have been produced more profitably. The same could be said of new lines of primary commodities for export and even of traditional export commodities within certain relatively narrow limits.

It would not have been enough, however, to place production for export on an equal footing with production for the domestic market. In the large centers, measures would have had to be adopted to facilitate imports of certain industrial goods from the developing countries, thereby giving these countries a greater capacity to import precisely those goods for which there is a greater difference in cost. In this way, a very useful division of labor would have developed in the industrial field, very different from the traditional pattern of trading primary commodities for industrial goods.

Until recently no serious effort had been made to establish such a division of industrial activities among the countries of Latin America.

As regards the second flaw in industrialization—the frequent absence of considerations of economic yield—this is largely due to the lack of a far-sighted policy, which was naturally very difficult to establish at a time when the countries of Latin America had little experience in that respect. The process of industrialization has been neither continuous nor regular. Pressure of circumstance has provided a strong impetus to it, for example, in times of import difficulties due to a scarcity of foreign currency or to the consequences of the World Wars.

On such occasions, restrictions were applied where they were easiest to introduce without upsetting the development of the internal economy, namely on imports of finished items, particularly consumer goods. Thus, industries producing such goods sprang up. The easiest course of action, however, is not always the most economic. In many instances the production of certain raw materials, intermediate industrial goods, or capital goods would have resulted in a lower cost differential with respect to the international market than was the case with consumer goods.

ECONOMIC ASPECTS

The combination of the first two defects in the industrialization process leads to the third: failure to strengthen the structure of the Latin American economy so as to withstand external fluctuations and events. For want of a proper division of labor in industry—as also in agriculture—the policy of import substitution has had to go much further than would have been necessary otherwise; and as the preference in respect of import substitution fell on consumer goods, this trend either ended, or is about to end, in almost complete substitution as regards such goods in the more industrially advanced countries of Latin America. Imports are thus confined to the raw materials and intermediate goods essential for maintaining current economic activity, and also to capital goods.

This has brought about a new kind of vulnerability resulting from the disappearance of the reducible margin of imports. When exports decline cyclically, inability to import essential goods has an unfavourable effect on the growth rate and even leads to a contraction of the economy.

Excessive Protectionism and the Latin American Common Market

From another angle, industrial protectionism has been exaggerated. Of course, protection is indispensable for industrial development, but in Latin America, generally speaking, excessive trade barriers have isolated industry from world markets, and thus it has lacked the advantages of healthy foreign competition.

This and the relatively small size of national markets have been frequently responsible for internal restrictive or monopolistic practices, which weaken the incentive to technological progress and the corresponding increase in productivity. As a consequence we frequently see in Latin American countries forms of concentration of economic power that are not the result of technical evolution, as in the case of advanced countries; on the contrary, they very often only hamper it.

Not always do our countries give recognition to the principle that free initiative and free competition are inseparable. I hope that the formation of the common market will introduce an element of sound competition through the gradual lowering and elimination of customs duties between the Latin American countries, and eventually lead to the lowering of duties vis-à-vis the rest of the world.

We envisage a broad, single market instead of the twenty water-tight compartments in which Latin American industrialization is taking place at present. But this needs time, and I am afraid that the policy just initiated toward the common market does not yet have sufficient boldness and imagination. What the Latin American common market needs is, precisely, the political decision to bring its creation about, not with rhetorical formulas but with definitive formulas quantitatively established.

Strengthening the Latin American Common Market

In what would such a formula consist? The customs protection applied by the leading members of the Latin American Free-Trade Association, established under the Montevideo Treaty, averages over 100 per cent, in addition to the manifold restrictions by which trade in some countries is still handicapped. I would be the last to advocate that these tariffs be reduced vis-à-vis the rest of the world without very careful study; but so excessive a degree of protection among the Latin American countries themselves is hardly comprehensible.

This is the first point to be tackled, and it is in this connection that the Latin American governments should adopt, through the Standing Executive Committee set up under the Montevideo Treaty, a decision as to the policy they intend to pursue. What is called for is a firm agreement on the gradual reduction of the present unduly high level over a definite period of successive years. The length of this period, whether the process takes eight years or fourteen, is not the important point. What is important is that the level of protection be brought down to a substantially lower average, for example, 10 or 20 per cent, and the acceptance by governments of a commitment to begin putting the reduction into effect at once and to complete it within a given time limit, while reserving the right to reduce or eliminate duties by degrees, and in the manner they may deem most appropriate, through a series of negotiations. Unless such a commitment is assumed forthwith, I greatly fear that these negotiations will yield only fragmentary and ineffectual results. Its assumption is essential, in order that in the successive annual negotiations the obligation to fulfil it may be distinctly understood. That does not mean fulfilling it blindly. The average-duty formula leaves room for the maintenance of some duties at a high level while others are abolished altogether; but in default of an objective clearly defined in quantitative terms, I doubt whether we can carry the undertaking through to the end.

I am not proposing anything so unrealistic as a commitment to embark immediately upon the elimination of all duties and all restrictions. I do not think this could be done in Latin America, and to attempt it would be to pledge ourselves to a leap in the dark. My opinion is that we should advance by stages. The first stage should be the establishment of the aforesaid practical and specific objective on the basis of an average reduction or of any technically acceptable formula; and the second should consist in applying—as was recommended in the 1959 report of the ECLA (Economic Commission for Latin America) Common Market Working Group—a series of measures that in the course of time would culminate in the common market.

Some apprehension is felt, however, lest the benefits of the common market be reaped mainly by foreign instead of by domestic enterprises. I share these misgivings; and I do so not merely in imagination but because I have seen concrete evidence that there are real grounds for them. I have recently witnessed a case in point in a large industrial town where an important industry, which had always been in the hands of nationals, was absorbed by foreign interests; and in my travels in Latin America I have had opportunities of observing many examples of the same sort of thing. These are very serious developments, which might become more numerous under a common-market régime, and in relation to which the governments must define their policy since otherwise the technical experts would find it hard to cope with the situation.

One of the basic aspects of the organization of the common market consists precisely in the establishment of agencies to give more forceful technical and financial support to Latin American private enterprise under the common-market system, irrespective, needless to say, of whatever each individual government wishes to undertake directly in the field of industry. This is a topic which needs fuller discussion than is possible on the present occasion. We have long maintained this idea, and, fortunately, it was taken into account in the agreements reached at Punta del Este. Yet it is very curious and very significant that little has been said hitherto on this point. The fact remains that at Punta del Este the governments recognized that Latin American private enterprise must be given the strongest possible international support, from both the technical and the financial angles, so that it can gradually reach levels similar to that of its foreign counterparts. The tendency in question, which is general and must now be given concrete expression, is dictated not by an anachronistic form of nationalism but by factors whose roots lie very deep. Economic development is basically a process of training and perfecting national aptitudes in respect to technique and production. We should do well to remember that one of the aspects of the Soviet method of economic development which, despite the system's immense political and social cost, seems to exert a powerful fascination over our younger generations may be summed up in the following principle: whatever a country's

ECONOMIC ASPECTS

point of departure, however great its technical backwardness, and however unstable its economy, it now appears possible that in the space of a single generation unsuspected technical abilities can be developed, if the population of such a country is subjected to a strict and systematic process of technological training. Modern technology has no longer any secrets. Even formerly primitive countries have learnt to grapple with all the manifestations of modern production techniques, from the extraction of petroleum and the exploitation of natural resources to the most complex patterns of industrial technology.

In my opinion, Latin America will never achieve an appropriate and politically stable economic development on socially sound bases, unless a considerable effort is made to develop national aptitudes in the fields of production and trade, by means of technical and financial mechanisms designed to supplement the activities of the Latin American common market.

Of course, foreign private initiative also has a big role to play in the common market; but it is highly desirable to create a proper balance between it and Latin American private initiative, in order to prevent unfavorable political developments.

The Latin American common market will reduce production costs and will eventually facilitate Latin American exports of manufactures to the most advanced industrial centers of the world. This movement will require a more liberal foreign trade policy on the part of these centers in relation to exports from developing countries. The greater our traditional exports and the exports of industrial goods in which we have comparative advantages, the larger will be our own imports of other industrial goods whose production in Latin American countries would still be relatively costly in relation to the levels prevailing in the more advanced industrial centers.

This expansion of international trade would have, therefore, an implicit element of reciprocity. I hope that the industrial centers will find it possible to grant trade concessions to exports of manufactures from developing countries without asking from them in return such concessions as might weaken their industrial development.

The Land and Economic Development

From what has been said, it is easy to understand how industrial development is complementary to the introduction of technical progress in agricultural activities. However, the system of land tenure that still prevails in most of the Latin American countries is one of the most serious obstacles to economic development. But the problem must not be looked at from one side only. Efficient use of the soil depends not only upon the reform of the land tenure system, but also upon the rate of economic growth itself. There is a close interdependence between the land and economic development.

Marked Disparities in Land Tenure

The land tenure system is characterized by extreme inequality in the distribution of land and of the income accruing from it. Most of the productive land is in the hands of owners of large estates, relatively few in number, and the remainder is distributed among innumerable small and medium-sized holdings that are usually too small to permit rational farming practices. Moreover there are large numbers of people without any land at all.
Some of the large estates are, of course, farmed efficiently. But as a general rule, because of their very size, their owner draws a substantial income without troubling himself to improve the farming of his land or encourage his tenants or sharecroppers to do so. Moreover, he has only to wait, and the value of the land will increase by virtue of the growth of the population and the

development of the economy. And this in itself helps to attract those whose object is not rational farm management but a means of protecting themselves against inflation or of evading wholly or in part the burden of progressive taxation.

The stronger this interest in the opportunistic investment possibilities of the land—rather than in making the best use of its productive potential—the greater will be the disproportion between its value and its immediate yield. And this puts it almost out of reach of those who are best qualified to work it. Herein lies one of the reasons for the existence of minifundia. The existence of large estates, the excessively high price of land and the shortage of resources inevitably foster this phenomenon, as the pressure of population on the available land increases.

Land and Population

The dissemination of modern production techniques is also very uneven. Progress has been made in respect to production for export in particular but not in respect to agricultural commodities in general. Low productivity continues to characterize production for domestic consumption. This is one of the most important strongholds of pre-capitalism. There is no other field in the Latin American economy in which the profundity and magnitude of the disequilibrium between labor and capital are more apparent. In Latin American agriculture, there is still a high proportion of the active population working on the land on a basis of scanty capital and very low productivity per capita and per unit of area.

This is a very broad generalization. The problem does not take the same form in all the countries of the region. There are countries or areas which were settled recently—during the second half of the nineteenth century—and in which the proportion of the active population in agriculture is relatively low, since the number of their inhabitants who went to work on the land was determined by the latter's productive capacity. In other cases, lands impoverished by centuries of cultivation are subjected to the ever-increasing pressure of a population which is multiplying at an exceptionally rapid rate. Thus the demographic factor so greatly complicates the problem of the inequalities in land tenure as to make it in some cases very difficult to solve.

Modern Agricultural Techniques and Development

The rate and pattern of economic development strongly influence the use of the land. The rate helps to determine domestic demand for agricultural commodities and the speed at which the population surplus is absorbed. The pattern affects the incentives to agricultural production. Both factors set a limit to the introduction of modern farm techniques and the expansion of production.

There are some branches of agricultural production in which demand has grown rapidly and has given the consequent impetus to technical progress. This has been true mainly of production for export and of import substitution activities. The farmer has surmounted the obstacles created by the land tenure system or has sought new land which he has worked on a basis of advanced and capital-intensive techniques. But in the remainder of the agricultural sector, which comprises most of the rural population, the situation has not been the same. Demand has grown more slowly here than the demand for other goods and services, and it has not been vigorous enough to overcome the difficulties confronting it.

To remedy this, state action to improve the use of the tax system, to redistribute the land, to disseminate techniques, and to furnish the necessary capital for their application was essential. Such action has not been taken on a scale proportional to the magnitude of the problem. Even the relatively slow increase

ECONOMIC ASPECTS

in demand referred to has often had to be satisfied by increasing imports or reducing exports or their rate of growth, with the consequent aggravation of foreign trade disequilibria.

Thus, the limit to the introduction of up-to-date techniques is set not only by demand but also by the capacity of the rest of the economy to absorb the rural population surplus.

This same duality is also apparent in the case of technical progress, which tends, on the one hand, to increase the yield per unit of area and, on the other, to reduce the labor force required per unit of product. The logical limit to the advance of technology is set, in one instance, by demand and, in the other, by the absorption capacity of the economy.

Redistribution of the Land and Surplus Labor Force

Redistribution of the land pursues the following two basic objectives: to relieve social tensions by improving the distribution of property and income; and to increase productivity by creating conditions favorable to the introduction of modern techniques.

Carried out on rational lines, redistribution alone may result in an improvement in productivity, since giving more land to those who have little, by making use of land left idle or badly farmed, offers immediate opportunities for an expansion of production. From this standpoint, it would seem essential to consider the position with respect to those latifundia which are efficiently operated. However well the land is worked, there is a dimensional limit beyond which productivity, instead of increasing, is liable to decrease. Within this limit, there would be no reasons to divide up the land, since other efficacious means exist of redistributing the income it produces.

But this applies only to a few large estates, and these as a general rule are not common in agriculture for domestic consumption, where the prevalent type of farm is characterized by highly unsatisfactory techniques and waste of productive land.

It is here that the problem of technical improvements and population arises. The greater the extent to which modern techniques are introduced, the larger will be the population surplus that must be transferred from the land to other activities; and the bigger should be the share of land assigned by redistribution to each active person remaining in the agricultural sector. In the case of countries which, historically speaking, have only recently been settled, the problem is relatively simple; and within a few years the manpower surplus in question may be productively absorbed by the economy if the rate of economic development is improved.

But the same is true of only a small proportion of Latin America's agricultural population. As regards the remainder, the existing surplus is striking in its proportions, despite the low prevailing level of technology. Technical progress would of course greatly reduce manpower requirements even if production were to expand at a rapid rate.

This raises the most serious aspect of the whole question of redistribution. The active population, at present redundant—and this is all the more true of that which technical progress would create—can only be employed very slowly and gradually in the manpower-absorbing activities if the rate of economic development is not intensified considerably.

The foregoing assertion is valid from the standpoint of the economy as a whole. As far as individual farms are concerned, it may well happen, and often does, that the capital used to curtail manpower requirements generates a notable increase in profits. The situation described is yet another manifestation of the discrepancy between advanced technology and the lack of resources for its assimilation.

Thus everything goes to show that when the land is redistributed a larger number of workers will have to be left in agriculture than might be needed at more advanced stages of economic development. Due allowance will have to be made for the stages in question, through the farsighted incorporation of elements of flexibility in the program.

This is a problem which agriculture cannot solve by itself. Capital is required in order to economize on labor in agriculture as in other activities; and it is also needed if that labor is to be absorbed without lowering the current productivity levels of the activities absorbing it. If sufficient capital for this latter purpose is lacking, it will have been worse than useless to expend capital on saving labor which is to be left without employment or at best employed unsatisfactorily.

In such cases, priority will have to be given, in agricultural research and in the dissemination of sound farm practices, to those techniques which increase the yield per unit of land, although in some cases the two types of technique are closely related.

Nor could this line of action be pursued without taking into account the growth of demand. Otherwise, the benefits deriving from technical progress would be lost to agriculture. It would not matter if this were to happen in the domestic market, provided always that producers retained a sufficient margin to encourage further investment. But if the transfer were external, a situation unfavorable to development would recur.

In other words, the capital available for economic development, and the proportion of the population that will have to remain on the land, constitute decisive elements in determining the size of the holdings which will have to be formed by dividing up large estates or combining small ones, with due regard to ecological conditions. This, of course, sets a limit to the application of labor-saving techniques.

Education and Technical Training

Other important transformations of the social structure in addition to land reform are indispensable to the full penetration of technical progress and the best use of human resources. Indeed, one of the most apparent manifestations of the anachronistic economic and social constellation prevailing in Latin America is the very small proportion of people from the lower social strata having opportunities for medium and higher education. This constitutes a formidable obstacle to social mobility, with a tremendous waste of human abilities, vital energies, and initiative.

We frequently stress in Latin America the spiritual values of western culture and the essential role of individual initiative in economic life, and I of course agree with this. But if one examines matters closely, one cannot escape the conclusion that at present only a relatively small fraction of the population has actual access to that culture and enjoys the possibilities of fully exercising their individual initiative. This is due not only to the acknowledged defects of the educational systems, but first and foremost to the outdated economic and social structure and the tremendous obstacles to social mobility which it embodies. The greater the number of those who, coming from the lower echelons in the social scale, arrive at higher levels of both general and technical education, the broader the scope of the system of individual initiative and the greater its impact on economic progress.

I have been asking myself insistently if the inherent shortcomings of the Soviet system of centralization of economic decisions have not been largely compensated by the active selection of men promoted by their methods of education and training. I am tempted to imagine the enormous results that we could obtain in Latin America if we could radically transform our educational systems in the light of our own experience and that of others in this field.

When all is said and done, the important factors determining the efficacy, the dynamic force of a developing country's economic system, include the gamut of opportunities offered to all its individual citizens, whatever their position in the social scale, subject, of course, to an inevitable process of change. Maximum efficiency will be reached only after the problem of primary education has been solved and the proportion of individual members of the various social groups enjoying the advantages of secondary and higher education is consonant with the numerical importance of the groups to which they belong. Such a goal will not be attained without progressive structural reforms.

This does not imply that under present circumstances it is entirely impossible to achieve notable improvements in education and bridge the obvious gap between the educational systems in force and the present and future demands of economic and social development. But complete success can only be achieved— and that by progressive stages—if the educational problem is resolutely tackled and at the same time a properly planned effort is made to remove all the structural obstacles to the attainment or maintenance of a high rate of economic development. Hence, the inescapable need for structural reforms. First, there are those designed to promote optimum utilization of the existing potentialities of the factors of production: in land matters, by such changes in the land tenure system as are essential if production techniques are to be revolutionized; and in industry, by the elimination of restrictive and monopolistic practices and the opening up of broader horizons through a Latin American common market. Secondly, there are the changes essential to the expansion of the productive potential by means of substantial and increasing investment, not only in machinery and equipment but also in the ability and will of the labor force to make the utmost use of these.

In all of this, international technical and financial assistance will be very useful and important to complement the internal efforts that must be made by the Latin American countries themselves.

The Redistribution of Income and the Accumulation of Capital

It is not necessary to explain how these changes in the economic and social structure will bring a better distribution of income, but the problem must be viewed from a dynamic standpoint. If the level of living of the bulk of the population is to be improved by redistributive measures, no static formula will do. The consumption of the higher-income groups must inevitably be restricted so that economic and social investment may be increased. But it is inconceivable that a redistribution policy could be applied for the purpose of directly and immediately raising popular levels of consumption without some sacrifice of such investment. The end in view can only be progressively achieved as per-capita income rises and its distribution is improved. What is required to increase it is precisely the expansion of investment by means of the above-mentioned combination of resources.

Even so, the progressive redistribution of a growing income cannot bring about a parallel increase in popular consumption. The upward trend of the latter must be slower than that of income, so as to raise the rate of investment until the level necessary for the maintenance of a satisfactory rate of economic development is reached.

Popular Capital Formation

Herein lies the most difficult aspect of the problem, in which a new approach is more vital than it is in other cases: how to augment capital formation as the pattern of income distribution changes.

ECONOMIC ASPECTS

Without capital formation on the part of the broad masses, redistribution policy will have adverse effects on economic development.

This is a matter not merely of propagating passive saving practices, but of stimulating active, popular participation in capital investment and, in a wider sense, in the task of satisfying the demands of economic development.

Origin of Major Disparities and the Problem of Coping with Them

As regards redistribution, in the course of capitalist evolution it has resulted from two forces, in addition to the economy's own momentum: the organization of the trade unions; and taxation.

The power of the trade unions is increasing considerably in the Latin American countries. But in some of them it is not yet effective enough to ensure that wages are adjusted correlatively to the increase in productivity. What is more, it has not been possible to correct the adverse effects of inflation. Here, in the last analysis, is to be found a very serious manifestation of the relative abundance of underproductive manpower in primary activities, artisan industry, and unskilled services. Its persistent pressure tends to preclude a rise in real remunerations.

But the reverse has occurred in some cases, where the trade unions have yielded their power in order to raise wages above the point warranted by productivity and the entrepreneurs' profits. The result has been the inflationary spiral, with all its pernicious and disturbing effects.

Incentives to Capital Formation

These circumstances partly determine the action of the state and place a greater responsibility upon it when the weakness of the trade unions leaves income distribution almost completely dependent on the free play of economic forces.

Through taxation the state may exercise a considerable influence over income distribution and capital formation. But, on the whole, it cannot be said to have made good use of its opportunities. In some cases, taxes have clearly come to form a high proportion of the economy's aggregate revenue, but only a relatively small part of the resources thus obtained is assigned to capital investment, the remainder being used to cover current expenditure in which social objectives are not always given the priority they deserve.

From another point of view, it is unusual for the high-income groups to contribute as fully as they should, either because the tax system is regressive or because tax evasion makes a mockery of taxation itself or of proper tax collection.

Furthermore, fiscal interests seem to have prevailed over economic considerations. Although investment is insufficient, the proportion of income that is consumed receives the same tax treatment as the proportion that is allotted to investment. Nevertheless, some reforms have been introduced with a view to stimulating investment and discouraging consumption on the part of the higher-income groups. This is an avenue which calls for thorough exploration.

It is undeniable that this tax differentiation tends to rectify disparities in consumption but not in the capital formation deriving therefrom. The inheritance tax is of course the ultimate corrective.

When the state, instead of taking this course, resorts to taxation in order to appropriate resources for investment, this does not mean that it is obliged to use the whole amount directly. The use of part of such resources for promoting private action through development institutions has proved to be effective in several countries. But no assistance has been forthcoming in this connection from international sources except on a very small scale. Nonetheless, Latin American private activity offers great opportunities for absorbing those resources through these or other suitable channels.

The loan of investment resources as a means of promoting the eventual formation of capital does not have to be confined to enterprises. It may also be extended to workers. This may turn out to be one of the most effective means of achieving popular capital formation and a question arises here which should be given some consideration. The use of credit for the purchase of durable consumer goods has been rapidly gaining ground in the Latin American countries. This is clearly a way to afford the broad masses of the population access to goods which it would be difficult for them to obtain in any other way. But this, in common with inflation, is a grave threat to saving practices. Perhaps such practices could be encouraged by credits for the purchase of securities by the workers themselves, either in the enterprises in which they work or in others. These possibilities should be explored· and the organizations that finance development might play a very important part in these new aspects of industrial democracy.

Loans for capital investment have so far been made direct to enterprises. A substantial part could be made indirectly, that is through loans to workers for the purchase of securities. Reference has already been made to the need for international credit institutions to devote a large part of their operations in Latin America to encouraging incentive on the part of firms and concerns in the area. These operations could be co-ordinated, in one way or another, with the growing participation of workers in the capital formation process.

The Latin American countries regularly face a very serious problem of capital formation in their public services. The use of international assistance for the purchase of securities in these services could have very important repercussions on the accumulation of capital and on the management of the enterprise. The participation of the producers and users of such services could provide a new way out of the common dilemma of choosing between foreign ownership and management by the state.

The Importance of Combining Internal and External Resources

We now arrive at a subject on which I would like to dwell because of its political significance. I think that a great effort has to be made in Latin America to mobilize internal resources. I am convinced that these efforts need to be much more intensive than is commonly supposed. If the investment required to accelerate development, with due allowance for the remarkably rapid rate of growth of the population, is considered in conjunction with the claims of education, housing, and public health, among others, the resulting figures will certainly exceed, perhaps in unsuspected measure, the internal investment resources that are being deployed at the present time. The greater effort thus needed implies a radical change in patterns of consumption, especially among the higher-income groups.

But the internal effort must be supplemented by an inflow of international resources much greater than that made available in the past. Otherwise, the rate of domestic investment would have to be greatly intensified, and this would mean imposing extremely severe restrictions not merely on the income of the more privileged groups, but also, I greatly fear, on the consumption and consumption increments of the broad masses of the population, to the point where very heavy political and social hardship might be involved.

That this restriction of popular consumption is possible is clearly shown by the experience of the Soviet system of economic development, but this experience also shows clearly its political implications. I have grave doubts that this policy of restriction of popular consumption can be maintained past a certain point within the present institutional framework. For the further one presses in that direction, the greater the need to employ measures of a coercive type, and the more they are applied the harder it will be to preserve the democratic system and institutions. Democracy, as we understand it and as we would like to develop and strengthen it in Latin America by adapting it to our realities, would thus have to be sacrificed, and with it, the inherent human values and ways of living, thinking, and acting.

The degree of availability of international resources can play a decisive role in this connection by complementing the internal efforts aimed at accelerating the growth of per-capita income in the next few years. This in turn, apart from permitting improvements in the living standards of the people, would also make possible the increases of domestic savings required for capital investment purposes. Were this policy of co-operation followed firmly over a period of years—not too many as far as the majority of the Latin American countries are concerned— these countries could then reach a stage where they would be able to generate within themselves all the savings they require to maintain a satisfactory rate of economic development, and they could achieve this without employing the drastic measures full of dangerous implications that I have mentioned.

The Political Significance of the Alliance for Progress

It is here, in my view, that we find the fundamental significance of the new policy of international co-operation embodied in the Alliance for Progress. Foreign funds brought into play in accordance with its provisions and principles should not be construed as an instrument to constrain the sovereign orbit of the great national decisions of Latin American countries, influencing their free determination with regard to internal or external matters. Otherwise, this would simply mean the dissolution of the Alliance.

Freedom, indeed, is indivisible; we cannot have one conception of it for internal purposes and a different one with regard to external or international matters. The political meaning of the Alliance for Progress is of another nature, and it has vast and far reaching consequences. It is an instrument through which the acceleration of economic and social development can be made perfectly compatible with the improvement of the democratic process in Latin America.

In general our democracies are rather void of true economic and social content and if we do not give them this content—and do so promptly without losing any more time—the desired goals of development and democracy may come to appear to the Latin American masses as the mutually opposed horns of a dilemma. I am afraid that if this happens the popular pressure in favor of rapid economic and social development will prevail over political considerations.

Internal and External Resistances

Let us not minimize the strength of the forces opposing the efforts aimed at giving a real economic and social content to the Latin American democratic systems. It would be greatly misleading to think that the acceptance of structural reform by Latin American governments at the Punta del Este Conference has paved the way for their easy and immediate implementation. However, let us not minimize, either, the effects of persuasion. Before the commitments contained in the Alliance were subscribed, it was hard to conceive the immediate possibility of some Latin American countries' entering into land and tax reform. However, these reforms are being prepared now, though not always with great determination. In some cases, the ruling circles understand the unavoidable need for these and other reforms and will act accordingly. In other cases, there is apt to be stern resistance. If this happens, then there is no other course but to continue untiringly the persuasive work until such time as progressive forces willing and determined to introduce these economic and social reforms finally prevail. Then the time will have arrived for a maximum deployment of the means of external co-operation envisaged in the Alliance for Progress.

But resistance to change is not only internal, it may come from external sources too. I am referring particularly to certain types of foreign enterprises that are an integral part of that outdated constellation of forces to which I referred earlier.

Although aware and in favor of the contribution of foreign private capital to our economic development, I am also aware of some cases where new and constructive formulas are urgently needed in this respect. I have in mind especially those cases of foreign enterprises which constitute real enclaves of an economic and technological character that are practically inaccessible to the people of the country, and also those other cases where they exert an undue influence in the national life.

Foreign Private Enterprise

The role of foreign private capital should be appraised not only from the standpoint of its direct effects on the national product, but also with respect to its contribution to the transfer of technology through the training of local staff at all technical levels. Considerable progress has been made in this field. The old method by which the country concerned provided only natural resources and labor, while foreign private enterprise had a monopoly of technique and management, is largely disappearing, although it still has some strongholds. Otherwise, initiative from abroad is usually an effective means of training domestic skills.

However, close examination reveals that foreign private investment has by no means reached the level that might have been expected in Latin America. Furthermore, much of this investment continues to be concerned with the exploitation of natural resources and with public services rather than with industry or farming. Yet it must not be inferred that the solution of the problem lies simply in encouraging investment in the last two types of activity. This would certainly alleviate the shortage of national savings, but it would undoubtedly give rise to other problems, and signs of these are not hard to find even now in some Latin American countries. The importance of this point justifies further consideration.

National and Foreign Private Enterprise

The technical and economic superiority of foreign private enterprise compared with its Latin American counterpart is not open to dispute, and neither is its importance in the transfer of technology. But this transfer operation is not enough; it is also necessary to encourage, in the country concerned, the training of local entrepreneurs, of men to organize and manage production, with all the attendant responsibilities. Otherwise, if a marked increase were to take place in the influx of private foreign capital, nationals of the country, because of their unfavorable position, would be unable to face the competition of their foreign counterparts either in existing fields of activity or in new branches.

There is no suggestion that the assistance of foreign private enterprise should be forsworn; far from it. But it should go hand in hand with measures to encourage the training and strengthening of domestic enterprise. In the absence of such measures, the unequal competition might well give rise to friction and antagonism which could easily take on a political complexion.

ECONOMIC ASPECTS

The measures that can be taken in this direction are various. The most obvious would be the establishment of a system of credits and technical assistance for domestic enterprises, so as to reduce and eventually eliminate the inequalities of capital and technology. There is a considerable potential demand for such credit, especially if it is not made conditional upon the principle that only foreign capital may be used for imports of machinery and equipment, and if operations are adjusted to the methods current in the Latin American countries, which are sometimes different from those in other countries.

Although it is true that the Latin American countries are not in general ready for very large-scale projects, it is equally true that there are a number of more modest—although none the less important—steps that they could take if such a system were organized. The rapidity and vigor with which imports of capital goods increase during a favorable export phase is enough to demonstrate the fact that this potential demand exists and could increase enormously if a persistent effort were made to encourage it.

In most cases it would not be necessary to establish new credit institutions, since use could be made of existing ones, private or official, that are sufficiently reputable and responsible to undertake such a task without the need for detailed control exercised at the source of the funds.

In this context, it might also be useful to extend the practice followed in some countries whereby local capital is invited to associate with foreign private enterprise on equal terms, or even to contribute a major share of the investment.

In other cases, very promising results have been obtained by provision of part of the capital from foreign sources, together with contracts for services to manage the industry during its first years, until domestic management skills are developed. There have also been strikingly successful examples of industries that originated as state enterprises and eventually passed under private domestic control, with respect both to the technical side and to ownership and management. At a less ambitious level where considerable success could nevertheless be achieved with proper organization, there have been co-operative activities of a strictly technical nature, involving concessions of the right to use certain processes and the granting of assistance against payment of royalties.

The Role of Foreign Private Capital

Foreign private capital has an important part to play in all this; but the question should be approached in the light of a criterion different from certain nineteenth-century concepts whose influence is felt even today. Foreign private capital, besides making its immediate productive contribution, must be a powerful instrument for the diffusion of technology: that is, it must help to ensure that the latter is assimilated both by the technicians and by the entrepreneurs of the country into which it flows, instead of remaining the exclusive prerogative of the foreign experts who introduce it. Once technology has thus been disseminated, these local entrepreneurs and technicians will be able, in the course of time, to emulate those of more highly-developed countries.

Unless an attempt is made to bring about this gradual and progressive technological levelling-up in the broadest sense of the term, the steady advance of development will be impossible, since the patent differences in training levels and the inaccessibility of certain techniques to local personnel will breed discord. Development will be neither economically sound nor politically stable.

Herein lies the key to the solution of more than one problem, since lower standards of technology give rise to understandable inferiority complexes, whereas technological levelling-up, by strengthening the idea of equality of opportunity, will make a noteworthy contribution to the fruitful association of domestic and foreign elements in the wide field of private enterprise.

All this is of great importance for the efficacious operation of the system of private enterprise. The Latin American peoples are fundamentally endowed with a strong sense of personal initiative, which has developed to a remarkable extent where conditions have been favorable. The significance of this for development policy is profound.

The Need for Planning and for Quantifying Targets and Resources

All this shows that we have to be prepared to encounter great difficulties ahead. We will continue to listen to doctrinaire arguments against state intervention and economic and social planning in Latin America and in praise of the supreme values of the free play of unrestricted economic forces. Planning and government intervention are not necessary to maintain the existing order of things, but to transform in an orderly and rational way the existing order of things. This is essentially why they are resisted.

Planning does not mean that the state will encroach unnecessarily upon the field of private activity, as is usually maintained. It is true that in the Latin American countries it is frequently necessary to strengthen the public sector in order to avoid the concentration of disproportionate economic power in the hands of private individuals, and to ensure instead its healthy dispersion; or, when it is necessary to do what private initiative is not doing, as frequently happens in our countries. But notwithstanding these cases, planning is perfectly compatible with the very important role that private initiative is called upon to play. More than that, I maintain the view that planning, coupled to a proper system of incentives, is the only way fully to utilize the enormous potentialities of private initiative and to give to it the dynamic validity that thus far it had generally failed to demonstrate in Latin America.

A development plan is a well co-ordinated group of efforts whose aim is to expedite growth, or maintain it at the same rate if this is already high, to make it as steady as possible and to improve the distribution of income.

Thus, planning means recognizing that the mere free play of economic forces does not by itself solve development problems effectively. But it is not the only way of acting on such forces; it is possible to envisage a variety of measures for stimulating development and eliminating obstacles in its path without the quantification of targets and resources that a plan involves. In fact investment can be encouraged by discouraging consumption, attracting foreign private capital, obtaining plentiful international resources for certain specific projects, and making a number of structural changes. Such measures could even be taken as a co-ordinated whole.

Would it be essential in such a case to quantify targets and resources? The reply to this question depends on two fundamental considerations: on the one hand, the limited nature of the resources; and, on the other, the time required for these structural changes and the accompanying capital investment.

The Limit to Resources

The limited nature of the resources raises a series of problems that need to be quantitatively analyzed before they can be effectively dealt with. These problems refer to: distribution of resources between consumption and investment; relationship between productive and social investment; balance between labor-saving and labor-absorbing investment; distribution of state expenditure; and contribution of international resources.

Distribution of Resources between Consumption and Investment

The starting point of a plan will be to raise the coefficient of investment. This would appear to be essential even when the rate of growth is satisfactory, in order to maintain that rate. The need is even greater in other cases—namely, the majority—where the rate is far from satisfactory.

This leads to the first major problem, which is how to reconcile the aim of a rapid rise in the level of mass consumption with the aim of increasing the coefficient of investment. In other words, how far should present consumption, or an immediate increase in it, be sacrificed in order to obtain a much greater increase in future consumption?

This question, which can be answered properly only if the data concerned are quantified, is of major significance, and will be even more significant in the future if, as is hoped, the share of the broad masses in income distribution improves steadily. It may be that measures taken to encourage savings in this group, as in the higher-income groups, will not automatically lead to the desired results. The state must then intervene in order to obtain the necessary additional savings, either by compulsory savings measures or by taxation. Or its intervention might take the form of increased governmental participation in capital investment.

Thus the state obtains, by means of taxation, funds that may be devoted to governmental expenditure, and not necessarily to capital formation. Hence, a proper proportion between what is devoted to these two purposes is called for, because otherwise the government would be exerting an unfavorable influence on the coefficient of investment and consequently frustrating the primary objective.

*The Relationship between Productive and
Social Investment*

Investment may be divided into two main categories: that which contributes to increasing productivity; and that which is merely reflected in improved welfare and has only an indirect and limited relationship to the productivity of the labor force. The first type includes investment in machinery and equipment, technological research and technical training; and the second, investment in housing, sports grounds, etc. The second type, which may be called social investment, is as essential as the first, but its volume cannot exceed a certain proportion without seriously jeopardizing the growth of per-capita income, which can be accomplished only by the first type of investment. Actually social investment is closer to consumer expenditure and may be regarded as a special category of such expenditure. Consequently, such investment must be governed by the basic decisions as to how far the objectives of the plan depend on restricting the growth of consumption.

*Balance between Labor-Saving and
Labor-Absorbing Investment*

After what has been already explained, it is hardly necessary to stress the importance of this point. As there is no automatic solution to the problem of the proper relation between these two main categories of investment, this question must be tackled at the planning stage. However, it has not yet been given much study, and further progress is required with respect both to its theoretical analysis and to the information available, before any course of action is undertaken that would have the desired practical effect.

Distribution of State Expenditure

There is a strong and persistent trend on the part of state expenditure to mount, not only because the functions of government continue to expand but also because of the actual redistributive pressure of income. This means that planning has to begin with the budget itself, as is already the case in a number of countries. This calls for a reorganization of the techniques of budgeting expenditure and investment, which at present are based solely on considerations of administrative or tax control. They need take account also of considerations of economic development, which are not, of course, incompatible with the other considerations.

The Contribution of International Resources

The calculation of the overall amount of international resources required depends on the total amount of investment needed to reach a given investment target, and also on the extent to which it is decided to restrict consumption, or the increase in consumption, in order to obtain the necessary domestic savings. Moreover, the total contribution of international resources must be determined in order to estimate its effect on the balance of payments, so that the necessary measures can be taken in advance to permit transfer abroad of funds for servicing loans.

The foregoing brief account shows that shortage of resources is one of the two main justifications for quantification in development. This shortage means that decisions must be taken as to how far present consumption, or the increase in consumption, is to be restricted in the immediate future in order to reach the economic and social targets of the plan in the more distant future. And it also makes necessary a quantitative study of the scope of these targets, and of the resources required for each of them, in relation to the resources available for the purpose.

Understanding, Firmness, and Patience Are Required

Be it as it may, we are initiating a long process that requires understanding, patience, and firmness of purpose. There will be many setbacks, many frustrations. There are no simple blueprints and easy formulas to carry out successfully the structural changes required, nor can they be conceived in the abstract and applied to every Latin American country independently of its particular situation.

Let us face the facts as they are. A few days ago, an American friend, a liberal and progressive intellectual who had shown sympathy for our problems, said to me bluntly: "I am disenchanted with the Alliance, aren't you?" "No," I said to him. "I am not disenchanted, because I was not enchanted before. I was never subject to any kind of illusions about immediate spectacular results. There is no magic involved and there is nothing that can exempt us from very hard and patient work."

I have found here some very well intentioned people who, because they do not notice yet any general movement towards tax and land reform in the Latin American countries, appear desirous of serious cuts in foreign assistance programs.

We have to look on all this with a broad perspective. This is a long-term policy, which should not be offered by installments or altered or readjusted too frequently under the influence of changing circumstances.

Persistence of purpose is essential, and any weakening of the lending policy due to too much impatience may discourage those in our countries who are fighting to introduce reforms and accelerate economic and social development. Nothing can be built solidly on shifting sands.

Need for a Promotional Attitude

Let us not be impatient. However, there are some forms of healthy impatience that prompt us to press for early and effective action so as to avoid unnecessary delays. When there is involved a great change in policy, as is the case in point, both the administrative machinery as well as the mentality of those moving this machinery have to be adapted accordingly; and this takes time. I fear that the larger the country, the longer the time that may be needed. This type of constructive impatience may bring forth good fruits. I would like, for instance, to see such good fruits harvested quickly in cases such as that of Bolivia. I was there recently, and I saw a country on the verge of despair, notwithstanding the great and promising opportunities for action that exist. This country has been subject to a severe anti-inflationary policy. This policy has maintained monetary stability, but at the same time it has been detrimental to the economy, which is operating at a very low level, with great unused capacity and much unemployment and underemployment, and is strained by serious social tensions. An immediate and vigorous investment program applied there might have considerable economic and social impact, and the Bolivian case could be transformed into one of the good test cases of the Alliance.

In all this we have to be aware of the dangers that would arise if the new policy of foreign assistance were to become a mere series of ordinary banking operations. This could jeopardize, or even destroy, the great goals of the Alliance.

It was hoped that countries would submit projects, and it is common knowledge that they have not done so to the extent anticipated. One reason for this is the uncertainty as to whether the requisite resources would be granted. A country needs to be sure that, once the figure for aid has been agreed upon by the international credit institutions, it will be entitled to avail itself of the amount, provided that it submits specific projects and has been carrying out the plan which it has itself outlined and on which the commitment entered into by the credit institutions is based.

But there is no doubt that a more positive attitude would also greatly help to remedy the situation. What is needed is a veritable promotion campaign to help governments and private enterprise to study investment possibilities and prepare the relevant projects. One of the characteristics of economic underdevelopment is the lack of proper administrative experience and organization for such a task, and international co-operation should begin precisely there.

In addition, international resources must be forthcoming at the right time. In some cases where this has not happened, it has made monetary stabilization policies extremely difficult to implement—as has already been seen—or it has helped to prolong certain critical situations unduly.

The Historic Responsibility Confronting Latin America

But we Latin Americans have also a great responsibility, which I do not hesitate to call historic. The Alliance is a dynamic formula for co-operating with those countries determined to use their will and power to dominate the forces of the economic and social process, and not to dominate men, dictating to them, from within and without, what they must do and what they must think.

We have before us the fascinating possibility of making great strides in industrialization with ample scope for individual achievements; of bringing about land reform and technical progress in agriculture, with freedom to own land through our own efforts. We have this and much more to look forward to, for all of this has ceased to be an inaccessible goal in this world of ours. Why should we have to renounce our political freedom to reach this target? That is the question that is being asked insistently in all our countries. We must give a clear and definite answer. We must integrate in a single and coherent system of ideas, the concepts of economic development and social justice, of active democracy and personal dignity, with all their inherent prerogatives.

We who are thus thinking are not alone. Let us all pay heed to that profound and ever-growing movement that is carrying forward our Latin American societies towards those unforsakable goals of man: a movement that may overflow at times to find once more its own fruitful channel; that at times seems to contract and to recede, but not to lose its essence and its vital meaning; on the contrary, to acquire in the very heart of the popular masses the overwhelming power required for great and sound economic and social transformations.

3

THE ALLIANCE
AND POLITICAL GOALS

Jose Figueres

TWICE IN MY LIFETIME I have heard the news: "The United States has joined! The U.S. has entered the war!" Those were anxious moments, first during World War I and then during World War II. On both occasions a world already embattled heralded the entry of a new fighter, young and vigorous, as the assurance of victory for the cause of freedom.

The Alliance for Progress may be considered as the third entry of the United States into an embattled world. In this struggle the theater of war is the Western Hemisphere. The battles are of a different nature. Once again, however, the appearance of the new fighter in the battlefield assures victory for the cause of freedom.

The Cause of Misunderstanding

How little we know about the back of the moon, our closest neighbor in space! How little the North American public knows about the war that has been waging in the southern half of this hemisphere during the last few decades—the war that the United States is now joining!

"Ignorance," in the original meaning of the word, "not knowing," "not being aware of," is still the main cause of misunderstandings in the era of communications. Ignorance still prevails in all countries. I once met an African student who admired Abraham Lincoln, "that wonderful chief who conducted the war of the United States against South America." Presumably Lincoln also preserved the unity of the hemisphere as one great nation.

I knew a lady in Latin America who would like somebody to explain exactly what the difference is between the United States and the United Nations. And I know a radio and television commentator in Miami who said a few weeks ago that the Latin Americans have been engaged, up to the time of the present Cuban crisis, in a cops and robbers game.

Yet for those who have been in it, this game of cops and robbers happens to be our Second War of Independence. It is also the war in which the United States now participates through the Alliance for Progress.

Sovereignty without Freedom

Our First War of Independence, between approximately 1800 and 1825, separated the present Latin American republics from Spain and Portugal. We became sovereign nations. Unlike the citizens of the United States, however, the citizens of many of our sovereign nations did not become free men. All our constitutions were democratic, but many of our governments were dictatorial. It took a century of education, a thousand trials and errors, and a Second War of Independence to establish democratic governments.

The Second War of Independence has been waged during the last fifteen or twenty years. Tyrannies have fallen one after another, giving way to progressively representative governments.

Whatever the shortcomings of some of the new regimes, they do constitute steps forward. Only three of the twenty-one Latin American countries are still ruled by the old-time dynasties and cliques. Peaceful means are now being sought to bring that era of suffering to an end.

The Latin American liberal movement of recent decades has established liberty over sovereignty; it has also laid the foundation for economic and social development. In sporadic actions at the beginning, followed by more co-ordinated efforts at the end, this movement has written an important page of our history, which is generally unknown in the United States.

It was only when one of our operations backfired—when one of the several groups which fought the Cuban dictatorship of Batista and assured the victory of the Cuban Revolution, had defected against the democratic forces to join the cold-war enemy in Havana—that many North Americans realized that the curtailment of freedom anywhere in the hemisphere constitutes a danger everywhere.

The delusion prevails in the United States that the present Cuban tragedy is the first communist attainment of power in the New World. Nothing is further from the truth. My own little country, Costa Rica, was the first American victim of the World Communist Revolution, from 1940 to 1948. It took a sacrifice of two thousand lives to overthrow a pro-communist government which had destroyed the electoral institutions in order to stay in power. Our struggle against communism was, unfortunately, launched at a period when the United States was a war-time ally of Soviet Russia.

The second case was Guatemala, where a communist-dominated regime was overthrown in 1954, this time with some co-operation from the United States.

Cuba is the third communist adventure, not the first. All the same, for my generation of Latin Americans the present struggle in Cuba may be regarded as the twentieth, since we admit no distinction between tyranny of the left and tyranny of the right.

POLITICAL GOALS

We have devoted our life-long efforts to protect the angel of freedom, and it matters not to us from what direction the poisoned arrows come.

The U.S. Should Know

We are not embittered or vindictive on account of the frivolous treatment given by the world press to a saga in which our generation of fellow Latin Americans has played an important role. Yet it is necessary for many North Americans to know that their new ally, Latin America, is the only continent that has been fighting vigorously and conscientiously for individual freedoms and representative government during the last quarter of a century. Some countries have fought for national defense and others for national sovereignty. We have fought for personal liberty and for the survival of the democratic political system.

It would be difficult to recount the number of deaths, prison years, exiles, and torture sessions that the men and women of my generation have endured. Comparing the personal histories of many of my comrades-at-arms with mine, I am ashamed to remember how short my prison terms and how mild my years of exile have been. I am grateful to recall how good my fortune was in combat. I am moved to observe how benevolent my fellow countrymen are when they shower on me so many of the distinctions that were due others who are no longer here.

As a non-Cuban, I hold the unique honor of having been in Batista's jails, and of having later confronted Fidel before his own applauding crowds. As a Costa Rican, it has been my privilege and my sorrow to participate, during the period between 1948 and 1955, in four successive actions which constitute the first breach of peace in our country in over a hundred years, and the first armed clash with the communist movement in the American Hemisphere.

Other Latin Americans have done much more. It is not my desire to exalt myself nor to praise my fellow countrymen. Rather I want to assure you North Americans that when you enter this Alliance for freedom, this Alliance for economic solidarity, this Alliance for general well being, you are *not* entering a game, and you are *not* associating yourselves with either cops or robbers.

A Realistic Alliance

Why is the United States joining in Latin America's Second War of Independence? For the same reason that the United States joined in World War I and then in World War II: because the instinct of the nation saw, yesterday and the day before as well as it sees today, that the moment had arrived when her own national freedom and prosperity were endangered.

For years we Latin Americans have wanted the United States not merely to help us, but to join in the fight against dictatorship and poverty. It is a Darwinian principle that no being and no species and no nation can be expected to act for the exclusive benefit of others. Self-defense comes first, or simultaneously.

Yet realism is no negation of idealism. They both walk hand in hand. North Americans who participated in the two World Wars, or who may take part in this new kind of war which is the Alliance for Progress, might be personally moved by the ideals of freedom and human solidarity. But the nation as a whole must be realistic. Its first concern must be the security of its own citizens. Its noble idealism must be channeled to the attainment of this realistic goal.

We Latin Americans consider this new Alliance to be realistic as a defensive move of the United States government. This is all we expect. This is all we ask for. Ever since Bolivar's time we have known that the well being of the Americas is indivisible. If the United States enters the fight with a view to the protection of her own freedoms, with an eye on the long-range interests of her own commercial growth, in the spirit of an investment and not of an expense, we are satisfied. We know that the sower is not the man who wastes his seeds in feeding the wild birds.

In the course of our Second War of Independence, for a long time the United States appeared to regard the attack on our freedoms as a Latin American concern alone. On this assumption the government of the United States ignored our plight. The people of the United States did not learn of our sufferings. The press of the United States disdained our achievements.

Under a policy of "business as usual" the investors of the United States were inclined to deal, and to induce their government to deal, with whoever was in power. Liberty and law, or tyranny and lawlessness, were unimportant. Neutralism ruled the day. When it was necessary to find out on which side some North Americans were neutral, often it turned out that they were neutrals on the side of "stability," which was a euphemistic allusion to the prevailing despotism.

There was a time in the United States when it required unusual courage, even heroism, for a North American in public life to stand for freedom and decency in the Latin American controversies. The sudden popularity of young Congressman Charles O. Porter in our continent and the lasting gratitude that my liberated fellow-countrymen feel for him are the result of his courageous support of our democratic forces at decisive moments. Now history is proving him right.

Economic Shortcomings

The author of the previous chapter, Dr. Raúl Prebisch, our greatest economist, represents several generations of Latin American scholars who have long stressed the need for economic programs and who have actually formulated such programs for the development of our southern republics. The Alliance for Progress is a tribute to their life-long studies and services.

Dr. Prebisch, whose learning knows no bounds, has, in his discussion, invaded the field of political analysis, permitting me, therefore, to invade the field of economics. Admitting that I do not know how to draw the line between economics and politics, I intend in a constructive spirit to comment on five economic shortcomings of the Alliance—which may be premature because these views are based on only a few months of observation.

1. Emergency Measures First. There seems to be insufficient realization that the Alliance is a belated effort. If it had come at an earlier date—for example, ten years ago—when the export prices of Latin American commodities were at a relatively satisfactory level, and when dictatorships were falling without being replaced by the communists, then the introduction of programming and the orderly supply of deficit capital from outside would have been decisive in starting or accelerating the process of peaceful growth. In 1962, however, after a long period of decline in export prices and of new political turmoil, the situation in most countries is so grave that they need *emergency measures first*, and then, or simultaneously, the application of economic programs. We are prescribing a wholesome diet to people in acute physical pain who urgently need a sedative. By the time we finish our examination and apply the sedative, if we apply it at all, the patient will have lost his faith if not his life.

Lend Lease was not conducted this way, and it won the war. The Marshall Plan took deficiencies and waste for granted, and it saved Europe. Is Latin America once more going to be the ugly duckling? No political stability and no permanence of democratic governments can be expected in Latin America today without immediate emergency measures of economic assistance. In fact, it is almost impossible to recapture the time lost. I respect researchers, analysts and bankers. But my instinct seems to tell me that on occasions we call on them at the wrong time. At this moment of belated efforts, we cannot take the risk of treating as a banking business what is really a war. This *is* war!

2. *Existing Business*. There is neglect of existing private business in the Latin American economies under the "terms of reference" of the international financing institutions. You may find credit for new projects, but seldom for the ordinary and mounting needs of thousands of reputable established firms. The advantages of the modern concept of "projects" are undeniable. But we seem to have gone too far to the extreme of what is now called "projectitis."

Some private U.S. banks have a more practical approach. They prefer to lend to established borrowers. But, (a) they have no satisfactory mechanism for obtaining guarantees rapidly; and (b) they do not go into the medium- and long-term credits that Latin American businessmen need. There is little realization in the United States that the poorer nations have practically no stock markets and no diversified savings which the enterprisers can tap. They are forced to use long-term credit. And banking resources for this credit are scarce in those countries, for the very same reasons.

When we speak of developing a country, or a continent, the assumption seems to be that we are going to start from scratch: an overall plan, plus shiny new projects. This sounds beautiful to the theorist, but it so happens that underdeveloped countries already have a functioning economic machinery. In fact those countries are underdeveloped partly because the existing machinery of established firms needs oil and fuel. Under the "terms of reference" of international banking institutions, our most urgent need, the need for refinancing, has become taboo. To those who lack understanding of our local circumstances, a firm that needs refinancing is considered to be in bad shape. You must have new "projects."

The next step in this direction would be to recommend to those countries that they discard the automobiles and trucks that they presently have in service, because, after lengthy studies, a few efficient Cadillacs will be shipped in.

3. The Magic Thermometer. The International Monetary Fund would be an even better institution than it is, if it were accompanied, as Lord Keynes is said to have wanted at Bretton Woods, by an international commodity fund. Since bankers have in our society and in our conferences all the influence that they should have, and since bankers deal in currencies and not in commodities, we got out of Bretton Woods with a good currency fund and without any commodity institution. This may have been the most fatal mishap in recent economic history. Probably underdevelopment would be a minor problem today if an appropriate institution had watched international commodity prices as effectively as the International Monetary Fund has looked for currency stability.

I knew a peasant who used to look at the thermometer and marvel at the magic power of such a small instrument to influence atmospheric temperatures. In our international business today, we expect the value of currencies to be the cause, instead of the consequence, of economic stability. Instead of preventing the price of coffee from dropping, as we rightly protect the price of wheat, we technically recommend austerity to the democratic government of Colombia, "to stabilize the currency."

Newspapers speak of political unrest in Brazil as "the cause" of currency devaluations. Actually devaluations and unrest are both effects of the ignorance of our era in the field of international terms of trade. At this very moment, international coffee agreements are being reached which, largely because of our own faults as Latin Americans, are sure to constitute a true stabilization of hunger. Austerity does not mean a little less butter for the people who have never been able to afford butter. Austerity imposed upon Latin America for monetary purposes usually means aggravated social tensions, loss of prestige for democratic governments, chaos, and eventual dictatorships from right or left.

You may say that this is a dismal picture and there is no solution in sight. Unfortunately that is nearly right. The Alliance for Progress will not find stable solutions until a thorough study is made of the commerce between the industrialized and the less developed nations of the West. This is not only a problem of commodity prices. It embraces the whole relationship between the poor and the rich countries, which is as inadequate today as was the internal relationship between labor and business in Britain in the 1850's.

Marx prophesied that the gap between the "exploited" and the "exploiters" would continually widen until the Revolution would close it. He would have been right if the economic tendencies had not been checked and channeled by the growing forces of political democracy.

In the eventful year of 1848 John Stuart Mill announced that the distribution of incomes is a matter of political decisions and not of economic laws. Political decisions, and not automatic adjustments, have established social justice internally in the advanced democracies of today. As an unexpected corollary, an ever-expanding market has brought about an ever-expanding production. The same process will have to be repeated in the relation between the proletarian and the industrial countries of our time. International justice will have to be established to the advantage of our countries by enlightened political action and not by blind economic forces.

This will call for a great deal of knowledge. Barbara Ward and other scholars are working in this field. We Latin Americans are obliged to give our contribution. An analysis must be made of the international phenomena that constitute important causes of underdevelopment in the world of today. In the meantime, the programs of the Alliance for Progress are in order, and the emergency measures that the accumulated evils call for are imperative.

4. Social Reform. The Alliance for Progress calls for reform in the social structures of Latin American countries. No advice could be wiser. No recommendations could better help the political groups to which I myself belong. Democratic social change has always been the basis of our struggle. Yet at this critical moment I would recommend some caution. In many countries the same social groups that have traditionally prevented change, with the approval and solidarity of the industrial nations, are still in power. Remember the Russian saying: "for centuries you have trained the goats to eat the cabbages; do not now suddenly expect the goats to guard the cabbage patch."

Under our circumstances, social justice primarily means higher wages. Higher wages in turn mean increased consumption. Increased consumption for our poor peoples does not mean enjoying a room in one of the palaces of the few rich. Rather, it means a little more food and clothing, and medicine, and small battery radios in the thatched huts. Much of this comes from abroad, and it has to be paid for in foreign currency. Are we prepared to meet the added burdens to those lean balances of payments?

Not to be misinterpreted, I must say that my party in Costa Rica has adopted a policy of increasing wages and salaries in accordance with the rising productivity of the economy. From 1953 to 1958, during our second term of office, we succeeded in elevating personal incomes to the level of productivity of the moment. Unfortunately since then the export prices of coffee, bananas, and cocoa dropped. I do not want to tell you of the hardships and the possible chaos that Costa Rica faces now. We are paying a high price for having anticipated the Alliance for Progress by five years in an act of faith in international stability and solidarity.

No measures of the Alliance for Progress can greatly improve the living standards of our countries until our dependence upon exports is considerably reduced through industrialization, which will take a long time, or until exports are stabilized at a fair level, which will take a long struggle.

Some of our countries may and should distribute land, which they have. All of them should enforce tax collection. But I seriously doubt if there is as much meat to distribute, as some North Americans believe, in the body of our tiny, privileged minorities.

The liberal parties of Latin America (and mine is one of them) are all for fair distribution as long as there is something to distribute. But we are not social agitators. We are engaged in economic development as a means to popular well being. Therefore, we have to encourage capital formation: not luxury, not waste, but indispensable capital formation, which inevitably means some degree of consumption sacrifice.

5. *Taxation.* We do not believe that our general system of taxation is as bad as some outside observers say. Whatever its obvious defects, our systems lay emphasis on consumption of nonessential goods, which is economically desirable. I feel a compelling need to tell North Americans that our consumers pay a $1,700 import duty on a Volkswagen, $2,200 on a Chevrolet, and over $200 on a small refrigerator or a television receiver. In some countries of South America these duties are even higher.

You North Americans disburse the bulk of your personal taxes at a government office, based on your paychecks. We pay at the store where our check is spent. What difference does it make? Whatever our reputation as tax evaders, and your reputation as tax avoiders, the store is certainly a place where no one can cheat.

Through these high consumption duties, overall taxes in my little country, Costa Rica, gather 20 per cent of the total national income. This is approximately the same proportion as you pay in the United States in different ways.

It is not the taxes that make the big difference between you and us. It is what you and we have left after taxes. Both your average and your minimum net income are around ten times the income in countries like mine, which is in the medium levels of the twenty-one Latin American Republics.

It is not my pleasure to express these observations. I am acting as the Devil's advocate. Those of us who have long struggled for something like the Alliance must now watch for its success. Perfection is the enemy of goodness. Government is the art of continuously choosing the smallest of several evils. Accordingly, let not our ideals of social well being conduce us to any situation in which we might have to share Omar Khayyam's regrets: "Indeed the idols I have loved so long have done my credit in men's eyes much wrong."

I confess that something strange seems to be happening to me and to some other Latin Americans directly engaged in the fields of production, social improvement, or politics. We must be color blind, because we see red traffic lights where our colleagues, North and South American, who work in the more technical fields of economics here in the United States, see green.

I know most of the economists in inter-American activities. For years they have been my friends, giving me their valuable technical advice while I have given them my modest political support. These scholars, notably those stationed here in Washington during these cherry blossom days, must think that I have become an alarmist on the Latin American situation, after having been a sanguine crystal-ball gazer a few years ago, when dictators were falling without being replaced by communists and when our foreign commerce was comparatively sound. I sense a strange feeling when conversing with my friends, whether they be North Americans or Latin Americans. It would appear that we look at things in different ways. Everything is fine in Argentina, except that an austerity government fell. Colombia is growing at a satisfactory rate, with a stable currency, though two weeks ago half a million members of the Liberal Party voted

POLITICAL GOALS

pro-Castro. Things are going well in Peru, under a decent government, yet everybody is jittery about how peaceful this June's elections will be. The economic growth of Mexico is phenomenal, but, in spite of great social efforts during a half-century of Revolution, two-thirds of the people are as badly off relatively as they were in 1910. Costa Rica is a stable little country, yet after six years of crops sold at low prices, 40 per cent of bank debtors cannot meet their obligations; hospital employees are not being paid; unemployment is rampant; and the next government faces a deficit of one-half a year's income.

There seems to be no end to the number of economic studies. Oftentimes you know where your shoes are tight and where they need stretching, and every week you get a new recommendation for a thorough analysis of the anatomy of your feet.

Things are quieting down in Venezuela, presumably of their own accord, though perhaps if it were not for Rómulo Betancourt, the Venezuelan oil wells might have been by now in Russian hands. Brazil is a giant, slowly and surely plowing its way with little to worry about; but to some of us it looks like a gigantic powder keg. The financial situation of Ecuador is normal, though the overall picture is as hopeless as the price of cocoa.

I have visited countries where there is too much credit according to the technicians, while industries and farms are laying off needed workers because they cannot meet pay rolls. I can tell you of countries where there is not enough food, supposedly because of inflation, and of countries where the currency is sound but the goods are unavailable. Never have I been so confused. This situation reminds me of the patient who was thoroughly examined by good doctors from head to foot, with the conclusion that everything was all right except his health.

Oh Lord, please make me wrong! I believe that the way to go about the hemispheric situation, if it were politically possible—which is a great "if"—would be the following:

a. Full-scale emergency measures, at the cost of some degree of efficiency, in the spirit of Lend-Lease and the Marshall Plan.
b. Long-range development programs and social reforms.
c. A thorough revision of international commerce, which will require a great deal of study, and which, I believe, contrary to some people's opinion, will still be necessary in the future, after the Latin American economies have been diversified.

The Problem Is Political

Many of you will be surprised if I say that the economic problem of financing world development is small, while the political problems are almost unsurmountable. When the European vacuum had to be filled after the Second World War, the economy of one industrial country alone, the United States, then half as large as it is today and having been strained by the cost of a great conflict, was strong enough to supply the deficit capital needed to rebuild the Old World. There never has been such a large or such a wise investment in prosperity and security for all. Today the combined economies of Western Europe, the United States, and perhaps Japan, could easily supply the development needs of the less developed non-Soviet world.

I could fill this book with figures to prove this contention, which is shared by the scholars who specialize in this field. One-tenth of the current unused industrial capacity of the West could produce the trucks, tractors, and factories that would start the wheels turning in all the retarded nations of today. One-half of one per cent increase in the overall output of the developed countries would produce all the outside push that is needed for the "take-off" of the world's incipient economies. It is not judicious to disparage scientific achievements, though it is provocative to observe that the cost of sending a man to the moon may be the equivalent of the capital needs of the whole underdeveloped world for a period of five to ten years.

Money and bookkeeping are useful inventions, yet when we lose sight of physical things and look exclusively at their symbols we soon get confused in words, mental habits and prejudices, and, even worse, in political entanglements. It is not dollar bills, nor bank drafts, nor the taxpayer's money that are needed to help industrialize other countries. What is needed are concrete mixers, bulldozers, and power plants—the things that can be readily produced by the developed nations at a small additional burden to their industrial plants, probably helping to stabilize their own economies at the same time.

The major problem is: How can you make people understand? This is primarily a political problem—in the United States, in Europe, in Latin America, in the entire world.

Latin American Politics

The political difficulties that Latin America presents to the Alliance for Progress and to the general understanding between the Americas may be partly traced to this: our countries, though widely differing among themselves, are still the type of societies common before the Industrial Revolution—an elite at the top and a large majority at the bottom, with a relatively small middle class.

In times of normality or stagnation, the elites may well express the feelings of their nations. Whereas in times of change or crisis, the elite minorities become more and more disconnected emotionally from the impoverished majorities. They lag ten to twenty-five years behind. Yet they continue to be the spokesmen of their countries in their relations with the outside world. Their members travel abroad, and at home they receive the visitors from the richer countries. It is practically impossible for most visitors to penetrate the "barrier of isolation" of our ruling class. Speaking with taxi drivers, who are an encyclopedia in most countries, is not enough. They are over-sophisticated. Domestic servants are under-sophisticated. It is not surprising therefore to find foreign journalists, foreign diplomats, and foreign businessmen making the same mistakes in their appraisal of a situation. In good faith they speak the language of the local oligarchy, and they repeat its errors.

Neither is it surprising that U.S. labor, through its international officials, has been generally right in its evaluations of Latin American political leaders and forces. On most of our issues your organized labor has been on the side of the angels, doing much to save the prestige of the United States.

A few professors called the Latin Americanists, a few liberals who are members of entities like the "Inter-American Association for Democracy and Freedom" or the "Friends of the United States of Latin America" (FUSLA), and some exceptional individuals, have turned out after years of being considered along with some of us as troublemakers, to be the true precursors of the Alliance for Progress. The bulk of North Americans, on the other hand, have had an interchange of ideas almost exclusively with people who are either inactive in politics or who belong to the small conservative parties. These parties, generally speaking, cannot be expected to carry out the reforms recommended in the Alliance for Progress.

Almost in every country we have reform-minded leaders and political groups who are not communist, but who are simply unwilling to sacrifice the pro-communist vote. In the past these coalitions have led to different kinds of results. In the late sixties they can only lead to communist-dominated governments. Such parties and such governments will definitely oppose the Alliance for Progress.

POLITICAL GOALS

Latin America's Liberal Parties

There are organized currents of public opinion in Latin America that have received scant notice in the United States and which seem to be a good expression of the democratic trends of the time: the liberal parties.

Political parties in general seem to play a larger role in Latin America and Europe than in the United States.

When President Kennedy announced the Alliance for Progress in a historic speech, twenty-three political parties sent him a joint message of appreciation and solidarity, which I had the honor of presenting to the President. These liberal groups, whether in government, in the opposition, or in exile, are the true representatives of Latin America, if Latin America is going to follow social development along democratic lines. Democratic labor is a part of this movement. So are some intellectual circles, most of the young professional people, and a large proportion of the technocrats. In some countries one-third of the entrepreneurs help the liberal movement while the rest of the business community is either indifferent or allied with the oligarchies.

Our parties have organized a small Inter-American Institute of Political Education in Costa Rica, to train young leaders in the answers of democracy to the problems of our time. I am a member of this Institute. We receive economic help from some liberal groups in the United States. We train 60 students at a time, which is all we can do, instead of 6,000 which is what we should do. We also publish a magazine, "Combate," which attempts to be a voice for the social-democratic thinking of the day, particularly in the inter-American field.

I believe that this liberal movement of Latin America, which is friendly to the United States, despite certain understandable resentments, is the logical vehicle for the political action of the Alliance for Progress. Belated as the Alliance is, it comes at a time when the generation of Latin Americans who have fought for freedom is still active in politics. If we fail to deliver economic development democratically, the new generation now at the universities will try economic development at any political cost.

In recommending the liberal movement, I am prejudiced and I am grinding my own ax. But I am willing to change over if someone can find a better tool to hack out a path for the progress of the Alliance.

United States Political Problems

Perhaps the major political problems of the Alliance for Progress will be found in the United States. The government of this country faces the dilemma of simultaneously leading a contented people at home, who tend to be conservative because they have a great deal to conserve, and a number of malcontented, allied peoples abroad, who tend to be revolutionary because they have a great deal to change.

The people of the United States are still oriented toward Mother Europe, which is commendable, and not to Sister Latin America, which is lamentable. This country inherited the English language, a great deal of the English political wisdom on internal affairs, and some of the English disregard for the Spaniards. Latin America inherited the language, the chivalry and the anarchy of the Iberian Peninsula, and some of its distrust for the British, who speak English.

Foreign aid is opposed in this country today on the same grounds on which higher wages and social improvements were opposed in 1900. The historic experience that a better distribution of the national income has made industry richer, and not poorer, is still not easily applied in the minds of most people to the distribution of world income. Although slavery and cheap labor internally have long been proved to be expensive for a free nation as a whole, cheap raw materials and services from the poor countries are still assumed to be inexpensive for an industrial nation as a whole. As a result, the citizens of rich countries are requested to compensate as taxpayers, through foreign aid, what they should be paying directly as consumers of foreign goods and services through regulated international trade.

The remedies for these long-entrenched and almost invisible defects of foreign commerce are not yet clearly established. In the meantime underdeveloped countries have to be helped with the transitory measure called "aid," if world tensions are to be kept within control.

The leaders and many of the scholars of the United States have a clear view of these problems, and recognize how small they are economically by comparison with the output of the free industrial world. But it will take time, even under today's diffused education, for the majority of the citizens of any great nation to become sophisticated in this field. Meanwhile the press and the Congress of this country, with increasingly numerous and praiseworthy exceptions, represent the average level of public opinion. This understandably makes the work of your leaders in international affairs an almost impossible task.

Western Europe's Part

Western Europe should share in the responsibility of Latin American development. Historic ties, culture and trade link our republics with Europe as much as with the United States. Although we have direct relations with the mother countries, the good offices of the United States are essential, especially in co-ordinating the efforts of what is really a triangular economy.

Looking to the Future

The success or failure of the Alliance for Progress depends on our ability to meet political difficulties in all our countries. The problem is up to the wisdom of our peoples. Two equally unhappy things may happen if the Alliance should fail. Stagnation is not one of them. One may be the communization of the Latin American continent, following the pattern of continental China. This would call for increased military protection of North America and Western Europe. The United States' bookkeepers would have to write off, among things of greater consequence, $12 billion worth of investments. We Latin Americans would have to surrender 150 years of struggle for freedom.

The other thing that may happen is the "Balkanization" of Latin America. Our continent may be divided in two political camps resembling a geographical mosaic, like Germany and Berlin, or Korea or Viet-Nam. For the time being the division of the hemisphere resembles China, with Cuba playing the role of Formosa.

You may think that I am trying to frighten you. I am! I am worried myself and I am not in bad company. Dr. Milton Eisenhower has said that the communist movement is spending $100 million a year in education and propaganda in Latin America. I ought to know what that means.

Let me say, in passing, that any course that Latin America may take, other than the road chosen by the Alliance for Progress, will cost the United States an amount incomparably greater than the Alliance in money, in human resources, and perhaps in more serious sacrifices. Moreover, the cost of any other alternative will mean, for the United States, an expense, a bleeding,

POLITICAL GOALS

whereas the cost of the Alliance will mean a profitable investment.

How are the Latin American liberal forces going to behave in this final phase of our Second War of Independence? Here I must be brutally frank. We are happy and honored to have the United States as an ally, but please do not take us for granted!

Other politicians can be taken for granted, but not those of us who have already sacrificed so much in suffering. I myself am convinced that the hardships of my friends and companions who are now in the Cuban dungeons and the plight of the Cuban people at large would have been lighter, in spite of a communist government, if the opposition to the Castro regime had not been so vociferous, so persistent, so heroic, and, unfortunately, so futile.

I understand the reasons why the Hungarian patriots and the Cuban invaders were not supported. And please understand why I am not inclined to encourage our peoples to engage in suicidal resistance in those countries where worse may come to worst. Tyranny is not merely an exercise in cruelty; it is a means to an end. The communist revolution has its objectives. Its repressive measures of cruelty must be roughly proportional to the amount of opposition that it faces.

Sufficiently it has been my lot to send friends on voluntary missions from which they might not return, when my conscience told me that the sacrifice was justified. I have paid too many calls of bereavement on soldiers' widows and mothers to look at heroism lightly.

After the original experiences of the communists in Costa Rica and Guatemala, where they were defeated, probably no country that falls in their hands in the future will be liberated by its own people without a torrent of blood. This is a world struggle, and not the struggle of any one of the Latin American republics. Though I have not lost my fighting spirit, it is not in my nature to recommend disproportionate sacrifices.

Unity or Failure

It is not out of unkindness but out of a sense of urgency and anxiety that I say these things. The writing on the wall is "Unity or Failure." Never could I be unkind at a moment like this, when my soul is filled with reminiscenses of an inspiring address on unity or failure delivered in Washington by one who could inspire; when I hear replayed inside me the melodies of a symphony which is all kindness and love; when the air is full of notes from Lincoln's Second Inaugural Address.

If, because of God's inscrutable designs, the North American people are not prepared to support their leaders in this great conception of the Alliance for Progress, and to make it possible for them to build the bulwark of Christendom and democracy that the Western Hemisphere should be; if it is Latin America's fate to remain poor or to adopt a heathen culture; then the Latin American peoples who have given costly contributions to the democratic system should not be expected to go into further sacrifices and to die for a civilization that the North enjoys and the South only craves.

On the other hand, if it is God's desire that the New World should be united in prosperity and liberty; if this fortunate nation joins the Alliance with a full decision of the heart, and her citizens share the greatness of her leaders; if we work together with a minimum of expediency and a maximum of principle; if loyalty is reciprocal; then, undoubtedly, we shall all be on duty, and the entry of the United States will be heralded as it was in the First and the Second World Wars as the final assurance of victory for the cause of freedom.

No sacrifice will then be spared. And no smallness of the spirit will deter us from sharing your glory, if your Kennedy achieves what our Bolivar envisaged.

4

SOCIAL CHANGE AND THE ALLIANCE

Teodoro Moscoso

Economic Development and Social Progress

A GREAT DEBATE is on among students of societal processes about the relationship between economic and social development. At one extreme there are people who regard economic growth—narrowly conceived as annual increases in gross indicators of economic activity—as the principal task of those responsible for the direction of the national economy. At the other extreme there are people who are overwhelmed by the emotional impact of seeing privation, ignorance, and disease and, therefore, think it the principal responsibility of government to provide the have-nots with most of the benefits of modern life, immediately.

The advocates of maximum growth rates seem to have forgotten that economic progress is not an objective but a means; that the purpose of increased production must be a better life for the greatest number.

Conversely, those who seek immediate improvements in the conditions of the underprivileged fail to comprehend that we cannot consume all we produce without limiting the opportunities for those who have not yet been born.

Most of the discussion and argumentation is taking place between these extremes. I would predict that whatever conclusions result from the debate, many of the theories that are proposed will not find universal applicability, since decisions concerning how much to consume, by what sectors, and how much to invest in what areas will be made in each country according to its own peculiar economic and political realities. In open societies where representative democracy is effective, these decisions are not reached quickly or easily.

The partners in the Alliance for Progress must find answers to these questions co-operatively. At Bogotá in 1960, an Inter-American Program for Social Progress was approved by the American republics. The United States pledged $500 million for social progress as an initial contribution. In Punta del Este in August, 1961, the Alliance for Progress was launched. The Charter of Punta del Este emphasizes that economic and social development are inseparable objectives. Some have argued that in reality they are the same thing viewed from different angles.

Let us turn to some concrete problems to shed light on the situations we face. There is a basic difference between projects such as building a road, a factory, or a dam, and services such as providing school lunches for children, giving mothers medical care, or building low-cost homes for urban workers. The difference is in measurement of the benefits that result from the activity and in the effects upon people.

In the case of investments for economic development, the objective is to increase the ability of an industry or a region to produce more and better goods and services. The effects on the economy are relatively simple to predict, while the benefits for individuals and groups are more difficult to discern.

In the case of social investments, on the other hand, benefits to the individual and the family are easily recognizable, while the effects on the economy are less predictable.

It is not surprising that controversy and confusion prevail even among the experts on development. Since we are forced to make choices among alternatives to get maximum returns from limited resources, it is imperative that we be aware of the inherent conflict and complementarity of our twin objectives. In Punta del Este the danger was recognized, and for this reason the delegates agreed on the importance of planning both for social and economic development.

Earlier this year an inter-American seminar on social and economic development planning was held in Santiago, Chile. At that seminar, planning officials joined with the Panel of Nine High-level Experts[1] to discuss problems of planning for the dual development objectives. It was generally agreed that transitional as well as long-term plans must be addressed to both types of problems, and that priorities must be chosen from the range of investment possibilities in both the economic and social fields.

I have no simple solutions to commend to those who have the responsibility of reaching decisions about the best utilization of available resources in each country. But I do want to point out certain realities of contemporary Latin American life that should be kept in mind as our plans are evolved.

First: there is a vast gulf in Latin America between the privileged few and the underprivileged many. If the present distribution of wealth in most of the countries resulted in a high rate of savings and in their availability for investment, then it might be argued that the income distribution should not be altered radically because of possible adverse effects on economic development. For the present, at least, the fact is that wide disparities of income do not result in high savings by the rich

[1] Established by the Organization of American States, pursuant to Title II, Chap. V, Charter of Punta del Este, to assist governments in the preparation of programs of economic and social development.

to be invested in their countries' futures. Instead, many of those who have been privileged by historical circumstances to receive large incomes utilize them principally for conspicuous consumption and send much of them abroad for investment in Western Europe or the United States, rather than putting the funds back into their own countries. In these circumstances there can be no justification for the existing income distribution. All countries want to increase investments. But in the United States we would rather not receive any more flight capital from Latin Americans, even if it might assist in partially reducing our balance of payments gap. We want to see that capital reinvested in productive enterprises in the countries of origin.

Second: Latin American development planners should recognize that in most countries social development has been permitted to lag. The growing deficiencies in housing, education, health and sanitation must be corrected soon and effectively. Ways must be found to reduce the production costs so that a greater number of people may benefit from each investment. And in that connection we note that the experts on planning agreed in Santiago that projects in the field of social development can be engineered and put into effect more rapidly than those for economic development.

Third: I wish to emphasize the necessity of going to the people with these problems of planning. A social and economic development program if it is to have a reasonable chance of success, must enjoy wide popular support. This requires that the people have an opportunity to participate in the making of decisions at an early stage. It also means that responsible officials in the executive and in the legislatures should take their problems to the people, explain the complexities of their task, solicit understanding of inevitable delays, and inspire the people to make the contributions and sacrifices that rapid modernization demands.

The Goal of Social Justice

The Alliance for Progress aims at social change not for its own sake, but at change designed to promote social justice.

Social justice is an ideal that is not new to the Western Hemisphere. It is rooted in the noblest traditions of our peoples and enshrined in our constitutions. It derives from our common Judeo-Christian heritage, and it has been affirmed by the sacrifice of our revolutionary fighters in war and in peace, generation after generation.

For us in the Western Hemisphere, social justice has always meant three things:

First, government of, by, and for the people—that is, a political system with the widest popular participation and benefit;

Second, the primacy of the individual and the family over the state—that is, the maximum degree of freedom compatible with national security and community organization;

And finally, equality of opportunity in all fields of endeavor— economic, educational, cultural and political.

In none of our countries have we achieved that happy state where we can say that social justice prevails. We in the United States are constantly endeavoring to approximate that condition. In some areas we have been most successful, in others we are still laggard. In Latin America the existing tensions, indeed the threat of potential violence, would indicate that, despite significant achievements in some areas, a great deal must still be done—if only to catch up with the admittedly still imperfect situation in the United States.

The Alliance for Progress is a historic, co-operative effort to accelerate the evolution toward social justice. Responsible Americans, North and South, cannot sit back and contemplate partial achievements in any of our countries while gross injustice survives in any part of this hemisphere.

There exists an unfortunate misconception among some people in Latin America that in the United States we are not concerned with the interests of the mass of the people in our sister republics. There is a belief that all we seek is the guaranty of our national security in order to enjoy the fruits of our economic advancement. This is not true. We realize that our own security and well being are inseparable from the security and welfare of our neighbors. Economic health and social justice in the rest of the hemisphere, thus, are a matter of the national interest of this country. But beyond this, the people of the United States share with all other Americans a fervent devotion to freedom and social justice for all men. We all lose ground every time the evolution of social justice is set back by the loss of liberty through dictatorial rule, every time an opportunity for social progress is lost. We cheered with the rest of the Americans when the Batista dictatorship was overthrown in Cuba, and we rejoiced when the Venezuelan people put an end to the Pérez Jiménez tyranny. But we also have been profoundly saddened by the betrayal of the Cuban revolution, which has made the citizen a slave of the state in the name of social reform, thus turning back the clock of progress.

There is an active emotional response in the United States whenever people anywhere go forth in search of social justice. We have seen its latest manifestation in the dedication and enthusiasm of the Peace Corps volunteers, and in the solemn pledges of the Charter of Punta del Este.

The people of the United States are not prepared to support a large-scale effort which they think will result in the perpetuation of social and economic systems that are structured so as to benefit the few to the detriment of the many. However, our people will gladly support that effort through public and private means for the sake of advancing social justice in Latin America. This is precisely why we are insisting on reforms as a condition of our material support to Latin America. We would rather withhold our assistance than to participate in the maintenance of a status quo characterized by social injustice.

Progressive Latin Americans need moral support from the people of the United States; they need to know that we want to encourage swift change in the direction of social justice. It is our collective responsibility to reassure our partners in the *Alianza* that we are behind their efforts, at every opportunity.

Some Implications of Social Change

Many Latin Americans will be told, during the next few years, that the Alliance for Progress is a scheme to replace the spiritual values of their Latin culture with Yankee materialism. It is ironic that they will be told this by people who themselves deny spiritual values in the name of dialectical materialism. In the United States we will be told, at the same time, that the Alliance for Progress is a scheme for financing socialistic projects with the savings of the American people, out of the profits of American industry. It is equally ironic that this charge will be made by people who will be among those to benefit from the success of the Alliance for Progress.

The success of the *Alianza* will bring profound changes in the Latin American way of life. The traditional class structure cannot survive. The vast difference between the few who live in opulence and the many who subsist in misery cannot persist. The gap between the highly educated few and the illiterate masses, between master and servant, and between oligarch and *campesino* must be substantially and quickly reduced. On these things the vast majority of the peoples of the Americas are agreed. Agreement that these things must change is part of the essence of the *Alianza*.

There are other social changes, however, on which there is less agreement—changes which are deeply feared but which are probably inevitable.

Let us first consider the family. It is unavoidable that many basic aspects of family life will change under the impact of economic development. The extended family of uncles and aunts, grandparents and grandchildren, cannot remain geographically intact in a single village, rural region, or city neighborhood under the pressures of a modern economy. As economic opportunity is provided in these areas, there will be jobs for individuals rather than for whole families. Fathers and sons will often become physically separated from each other in the very process of finding more productive and satisfying ways to earn their living. This does not necessarily mean that family ties have to be harmfully weakened, just because family members live farther apart. The new jobs which draw them physically apart will also cumulatively provide the means of transportation and communication which can bring them back together again.

But deeper aspects of family life than mere physical proximity are threatened by economic progress. Poor and uneducated parents will have a hard time retaining the respect of children who know the modern world better than they. Men will not appreciate having their traditional authority challenged by women who earn nearly as much as they do. The extended family will suffer from the loss of many of its traditional functions. The role of providing insurance, medical care, schooling, and entertainment will pass increasingly from the family to more specialized institutions.

Many Latin Americans fail to realize that they are not alone in their reverence for the family and in their regret at the strains that modern life places upon it. Perhaps they are not fully aware that North American families have suffered these same strains in this generation—immigrant families whose children have lost their parents' language, farm families whose younger members have left the farm for the city, workers' families whose children have entered the professions. The preservation of the family is not a Latin American but a global problem—one which North Americans have faced somewhat earlier and which they still have not resolved completely. If Latin Americans are more aware of the failures than the successes of the U.S. family in its battle with the demands of modern life, this is only because these failures are more obvious and better publicized than the accomplishments. Latin Americans are determined to preserve the integrity of the family. For this they will be admired in the United States. But they will also come to feel a greater sympathy with us as they themselves face the forces which have already posed problems for the family in the United States.

A problem closely allied to that of the family is the movement of people from the country to the city. In the United States, less than 10 percent of the working population make their living from the land. For every agricultural worker there are ten workers producing non-farm goods and services for which the agricultural worker can exchange his produce. In Latin America there is less than one urban worker for every worker on the land. Many programs are under way in Latin America to improve the lot of the people on the land, and to reduce the explosive growth of city slums. However, our best efforts will no more than slow the tide and thus give us more time to create city jobs, build homes, and provide city services. We cannot stop the movement to the city, nor do we want to, but we can help provide for rural families many of the services and facilities available in the city, thereby reducing the disparity between rural and urban life. And we recognize that the *campesino* cannot be emancipated through land redistribution programs alone. Without credit, education, technical advice, machinery, electricity, new markets, and roads, the partitioning of land—the mere passing of titles—will not transform the *campesino* into an agricultural entrepreneur.

The Basic Role of Education

The most important device at our disposal for achieving orderly social revolution in Latin America—rural and urban—is education.

I do not mean only traditional education in the humanities and basic sciences, but education which enhances the individual's ability to find better-paid work.

A worker's productivity—and thus his income—can, of course, be increased indirectly by providing him with more and better capital. The productivity of a farmer can be raised if he gets better land or modern implements; a factory worker will be more productive if he is given improved machinery in a newer plant. However until recently there has been insufficient understanding of the vital contribution to economic development that can result from an upgrading of the labor force. Fortunately, educational investments contribute at the same time to economic and social development.

For example, if the child of a poor rural or urban family reaches adulthood in a state of semi-literacy, the chances are that his future income will be not much higher than that of his father. This will mean that his capacity to provide his own children with a better life, and to help his parents in their old age, will be severely limited. The burden upon the rest of society will be that much greater. If, instead, that child can be trained as a technician, a teacher, or a scientist, his income-earning capacity will have been enhanced. By raising his family's standard of living he will not only reduce the burden on society; he will actually be able to carry a share of the social burden for others. In the process he will have contributed to economic development by raising national output. Incidentally, he will also have become a better citizen and perhaps even a leader in his community.

Recognizing the importance of education for economic and social development is, however, only the beginning. Many intricate problems remain. Should the emphasis be on technical education and at all levels, or just at the university level? Should the country embark on a program of improved primary and secondary education for all children? If so, the economic consequences will not be felt for several years. Should educational resources be concentrated on upgrading the skills of those already in the labor force?

There are no general answers to these questions. Each country must assess its manpower and educational situation and decide how and when to utilize its scarce resources. In Latin America, increasing attention will have to be given to manpower planning, so that investments in social capital will give maximum returns in human as well as economic terms. Within the Alliance for Progress, education at all levels and in all categories will be stimulated.

In the spring of 1962, educational leaders of all of the nations of the Western Hemisphere met in Santiago, Chile, and resolved that by 1970 all children from 7 to 14 years of age should have school facilities. This is a difficult but feasible objective, as are the similarly ambitious goals adopted for secondary and university education.

Manpower Problems

Another important result of the Santiago conference was the decision to begin in September, 1962 an intensive course for Latin American officials concerned with education and manpower problems. For this purpose a new Division of Human

Resources Development is being added to the Latin American Institute of Economic and Social Development which will open its doors to students in Santiago. The Alliance for Progress is encouraging and supporting the work of the Institute.

The manpower problem of Latin America would not be resolved, however, even if it were possible to expand primary, secondary and university enrollment to its optimum by 1963. Many knowledgeable and perceptive Latin American leaders believe that the first task of the *Alianza* should be to address itself to the 50 million underprivileged adults of Latin America. They are people without education or skills useful in the modern world—people who have not been fully integrated into the national production or political systems and, therefore, cannot identify themselves with the aims and aspirations of their respective countries.

Educational problems in the developing countries are further complicated for the immediate future by declining infant mortality rates. A greater proportion of Latin American children reach school age each year than ever before. They outnumber their parents and grandparents combined. There are almost as many children of school age in Latin America as there are adults of working age. Every Latin American worker today has to support twice as many school age children as his fellow worker in Europe or the United States. This condition is temporary. It will last only as long as it takes the present generation to grow up and would correct itself even if birthrates were to remain high.

The comparative youth of the Latin American population presents an obstacle to development as well as an opportunity for rapid change. The race between increased output and the steep increase of consumers is presently going against the Latin American countries. On the other hand, while the consumer demands of youthful populations limit the accumulation of savings for investment, the very existence of this reserve of human resources represents a tremendous potential for economic development and social change. If Latin Americans can use the next few years to provide their children with educational tools and techniques, they will receive vast dividends in economic growth. If, on the other hand, the opportunity is lost or misused, the resulting frustrations of the people will provide fertile grounds for experimentation with radical extremism.

A Sense of Urgency

One of our principal tasks in the Alliance is to infuse a sense of urgency in high places—an awareness of the pressure of time under which we are working. The peoples of Latin America are impatient, and justifiably so. They are tired of waiting for that happy tomorrow, that timeless *mañana*. They are demanding a better life today. If those now in strategic positions do not make wise decisions quickly, there will be a push to concentrate policy and power in the hands of the extremist minorities. The result could be social development without economic growth, or economic development without social justice.

The loss of freedom is too high a price to pay for economic growth. Economic stagnation is too high a price for social justice. Under the Alliance for Progress we are determined to pursue both, and we, the Americans of the North and South, intend to succeed.

5

THE ALLIANCE IN THE CONTEXT OF WORLD AFFAIRS

Dean Rusk

THE ALLIANCE FOR PROGRESS represents the most important common venture in the long history of our hemisphere. On its success depends the individual welfare of hundreds of millions our people—the independence and freedom of many of our nations—and the continued flourishing of that civilization which our ancestors built in the wilderness and which their successors have struggled to bring to full flower.

For us, the Alliance is a special part of an indivisible whole. It rests on those indissoluble ties of geography and history, of common culture and common interest, which have always bound the American nations together. It rests on the realization that this hemisphere is part of that Western civilization which we are struggling to protect; that many of the highest values of that civilization have found their richest expression in the life of the nations to the South. It rests on the special responsibilities of the United States in this hemisphere—responsibilities which exist independently of the cold war, or a Soviet military threat or the demands of nations newly freed from colonial rule. It is an Alliance which my country has joined because of our realization that the destiny of the United States is irrevocably joined to the destiny of our sister republics of the New World.

Freedom of Men and Nations

The basic goal of American foreign policy is a world where individual men are free to pursue their own ends, subject only to the liberating restraints of a free society. It is significant that this is a policy whose central focus is man and not the governments which rule him. For such a policy rejects the thesis that the state is the end of human striving—the ultimate product of individual effort. Thus it rejects a way of life which is as ancient as the tyrannies of the dawn of history and as modern as the communes of Communist China. Of course this policy is limited by the fact that we must act as a government; and in the sphere of international relations our dealings must, for the most part, be with other governments. Thus we must guide our efforts toward the support and strengthening of societies which share our basic goals for man. This policy, too, must at times take account of the realities of the world conflict; of the presence of a powerful adversary who seeks to destroy the framework of freedom which we are laboriously constructing. But none of the detours or delays which may be forced upon us will take us far off course if we keep in mind the basic guiding principles of our policy.

Each generation is called upon to write its own chapter in the long and stimulating story of freedom. In the world as it is today, the chapter which we are called upon to write involves both strength for defense against aggression and a mighty creative effort to build a decent world order. The United States has accepted, as a matter of necessity, the maintenance of a military force of such undeniable power that no rational decision could be made to attack the free world. It is a burden we gladly bear and would as gladly lay aside as soon as possible. We know that security does not lie in an unlimited arms race, and we have made sober and persistent efforts to turn that race downward and to strengthen the processes of peace. Although there are discouragements, we shall continue that effort because we understand that it is no simple matter to transform the nature of international relations overnight. But the transformation must come. Meanwhile, we shall do our part to provide the strength which is required in the actual world in order to give us a chance to bring into being another kind of world required by the nature and destiny of man.

The second part of our grand design is our readiness to contribute in every appropriate way to the building of free, politically stable and independent nations. Although we cannot guarantee that these states will always share our hope for the future of man, it is clear that this hope can only be realized within such a society. Only such a society can resist efforts at subversion and revolt promoted from without. Only such a society is secure enough to grant enlarging individual liberties to its citizens. Only such a society can hope to carry forward the prodigious task of development on which the welfare of its people, as well as its future stability, so largely depend.

The instruments with which we carry forward this part of our policy are far more complex and subtle than even the most ingenious techniques of modern military strength. But basically they rest on the encouragement and strengthening of two forces which are products of our Western civilization: political freedom, national and individual; and the drive toward economic development.

It was here in this hemisphere that men first broke the bonds of colonial rule, destroyed alien rule on this continent, demanded the right of self-determination, and fought to establish that right. It was Washington and Bolivar, Jefferson and San Martin, who first gave national expression to the forces which today guide the struggles of men across turbulent Africa and Asia. This nationalism is the strongest political force of the modern world. And in all corners of the world international communism struggles to break it down, to impose an international discipline which merely means the substitution of new colonial masters for the old. But since 1776 no nation has been able successfully to destroy the force of nationalism and, indeed, today we are witnessing its pervasive effect on the communist empire itself.

Thus we welcome and support the new nations of the world. We encourage them in their efforts to achieve national independence and to express their legitimate national interest. For we who have established a pluralistic national society do not share the communists' fear of the confusions, the uncertainties, and the liberating discords of a pluralistic world society. In this it is we, and not the communists, whose national goals ride with the events of history.

Economic Development and a Free Society

The drive toward economic development is essentially a product of the Western technological revolution. It was this revolution that has provided man with the capacity to emerge from centuries of poverty and hunger and ignorance. And it was also this revolution that awakened man's realization that such capacity was within his grasp.

Suddenly, in the years following World War II, it became apparent that the vast unbridgeable gulf between the rich and poor nations had become a wall of glass. On one side of that wall were the capital, the scientific advances, the technological skills of the industrialized nations; and on the other, the poverty and hunger and the fierce desire for a better life of the great masses of the underdeveloped continents. The shattering of that wall, the application of the tools and wealth of the industrialized nations to the needs of the poorer nations became, and still remains, the central issue of our time. We have confronted this problem with the new tools of economic aid, national planning, and social reform. Yet it is clear that the successful completion of this task will require new breakthroughs of thought and action—the devising of new tools and techniques for the creation of capital and credit, for trade and the spread of technology. We will have to look afresh at all the institutions and procedures we have developed to speed up growth within each country of wealth and productive capacity. For only new efforts of imagination and intellect will enable us to shatter the glass wall and liberate the undoubted capacity of our society to bring, and bring rapidly, a better life to man.

For the past fifteen years the United States has devoted itself to assisting the economic development of other nations. That development is central to the basic goal of our foreign policy. First, because it will provide the material welfare necessary to liberate the skills and capacities of individual men, and to give them an opportunity for the exercise of freedom. And, second, because, in today's world, only a nation which is making steady economic progress, and offering hope and a realization of that hope to its people, can maintain the political stability essential to the maintenance of its national integrity and political liberty. For it remains true that governments derive their just powers from the consent of the governed.

In the harnessing and encouragement of this second great force—the drive toward economic development—free societies possess a great advantage. For it is the free societies that first set loose this force; that first developed the technological capacity to improve the material welfare of man; that first illuminated the prospects of a better and more abundant life for the people of the world. It is our science, our methods of distribution, and our economic techniques that have lifted man into the industrial age. The history of the past twenty years has demonstrated clearly that economic development can best be achieved within the context of a free society unhampered by the ponderous arrangements of a nineteenth-century Marxist doctrine framed for another age and another set of conditions.

At the close of World War II many nations, their economies shattered by the war, began the task of reconstruction and economic growth. Some began this development within the constitutional framework of a free society. Others, subjugated by military conquest or armed revolution, took the communist road to economic progress. Today, seventeen years later, the results are becoming clear. They can be seen in the dramatic picture of a free, prosperous Western Europe confronting the drabness of Eastern Europe. They can be seen in the performance of Japan, which has reached new heights of prosperity as the fastest growing nation of the world, over against the hunger and starvation which afflict the vast population of China. And they can be seen in Cuba where the decline in agricultural production, the food rationing, and the drop in real incomes illustrate the emptiness of communist claims to rapid development.

We take no satisfaction from economic distress under whatever system it exists. But it is relevant to point out that communist techniques have not produced the promised results despite appalling prices in human values paid for economic development.

During the 1950's after basic war damage had been largely repaired, the Soviet Union's economy grew at a rate of $6\frac{1}{2}$ per cent; it was a good performance, but it was exceeded by many free countries, including Germany, Austria, Japan, and Venezuela. Even with a slower rate of growth, the United States during the 1950's increased the absolute gap between its economy and that of the Soviet Union. At current projections for 1961–1970, the absolute gap will continue to widen as the United States adds more than $300 billion to its annual GNP, while the Soviets add a possible $170 billion to theirs.

All told, over the next nine years, the nations of the Sino-Soviet bloc can expect to add $300 billion to their GNP, while the nations of the Atlantic community and Japan will add more than $500 billion.

These figures, even with allowances for the vagaries of statistical analysis, clearly demonstrate that no communist society has found a magic formula for economic growth; and that rapid progress can readily be achieved by a free society.

Even more important than the statistics of economic growth are the uses to which this increased abundance has been put. For our aim is to improve the welfare of people—to relieve human want and misery—not merely to pursue increased output as an end in itself. The economic history of the communist bloc is a clear and dramatic proof that the communist route to development, effective as it may be in increasing national power, is the least effective means of raising the living standards of individual men and women.

This is most dramatically illustrated in the Soviet Union itself, the focal point and pride of communist development.

Most significant has been the sluggish performance of communist agriculture. Throughout the entire communist world the doctrines of Marx have been proven incapable of mastering the techniques of modern food production and providing an abundant diet.

Almost half of the Soviet work force is engaged in agriculture as compared with nine per cent of the American work force. But the average American, according to the Department of Agriculture, has at his disposal three times as much fresh fruit, eggs, and edible fats and twice as much meat and sugar as the average Soviet citizen.

In recognition of this agricultural problem, Chairman Khrushchev recently warned—thirty years after collectivization—that "the entire economy can be wrecked if the lagging of agriculture is not noticed and overcome in time."

Across the communist world the story is the same. Eastern Europe, which in prewar years was a net exporter of grain, has in recent years had to import 5 million tons of grain. Production of grain in Communist China in 1960 was actually less than in 1957, although the population increased by almost 60 million.

In other vital areas the failure of communist economies to meet the basic needs of human welfare has been dramatic. The real wages of nonagricultural workers in the Soviet Union in 1958 were calculated at 95 per cent of their wages in 1928—a decline of five per cent over a period of thirty years. At the end of 1960 the housing space available to the average Soviet urban dweller was about equal to what he had under the Tsars. Other consumer durables are even scarcer, making it clear that the promised abundance of Soviet communism is still far in the future.

In the rest of the communist bloc, economic growth has not been translated into higher standards of living. In Czechoslovakia, the most prosperous of the Eastern European countries, it took the average industrial worker in 1957 longer to earn enough to buy a pound of butter than it took him in 1937. Only Czechoslovakia among these countries has an average living space greater than the nine square meters established as a minimum by nineteenth-century hygienists. In China and North Viet-Nam, millions are struggling to avoid starvation on subsistence incomes, with other comforts forgotten.

Behind these statistics and comparisons, lie two central facts: that communist societies are not capable of more rapid economic growth than free societies; and that they are far less able to translate growth into substantial increases in human welfare.

To those whose desire for development stems from concern for the welfare of the individual, and not solely from desire for national power, it is clear that the path of freedom offers the best and most effective route to progress.

Thus the second great force of our era—the drive for economic development—finds its best model and exemplar in those free societies which gave it birth.

However, the free nations are now faced with the problem of evolving a set of policies and tools which will enable us to carry forward the same development in the rest of the world.

The Inter-American Experience

The Alliance for Progress represents just such an evolution of methods and aims. Although the Alliance springs from the special relationships between the American nations, it embodies basic principles of development which are of broader application. It is a product of the experience both of Latin America and of the United States since World War II—a period during which the United States has devoted greater resources to the assistance of others than any other nation in the history of the world. These resources have helped to sustain economies in many parts of the world, have met emergency human needs, and assisted nations to launch programs of development. Yet we must also admit that some of this money has been ineffective. Some of it has disappeared without a trace of permanent effect on the lives of the people it was meant to help. It was this experience that taught us that solid development is not possible without at least three basic conditions.

First, no nation can develop unless it possesses its own inner determination to progress. This means the mobilization of national resources and energies, the use of national institutions, and, above all, an intangible dedication of national spirit and will—a singlemindedness of purpose, and an unrelenting determination which is essential to all great human achievements. If this condition is present, then external resources can give a vital, if marginal, boost. If it is not present, then no amount of external help will leave any permanent trace on the life of the nation.

No free nation will demand of its people the sacrifices which the communist nations demand—the loss of liberty and the rigorous regimentation of daily life. Such sacrifices destroy the goal of freedom for man; they are unnecessary even in economic terms and do not yield progress. But neither can we make the assumption that economic development is painless; that it can be achieved without arduous labors and sacrifice. It may require increased taxes, or the yielding up of large estates, curbs on consumption, or the barring of luxury imports. But such sacrifices are mild indeed compared to the communist alternatives, and they will ultimately yield greater abundance for all.

This first condition, under the name of self-help, is an essential component of the Alliance for Progress and of economic development everywhere.

With this in mind it is heartening to see the many examples which the nations of this hemisphere have given of their effort and will to improve the welfare of their people. These examples are not only significant in themselves, but they indicate the strength of spirit which characterizes this hemisphere and which holds such high promise for the far greater effort ahead. Let me cite a few of these examples of self-help and co-operation among the American republics—examples which antedate the Alliance for Progress.

Local Colombian initiative led to the formation of the Colombian Technical Institute, aimed at developing badly needed technical and scientific skills for all Latin America.

The Mexican Ministry of Agriculture has developed one of the finest institutes of agricultural research in the world. Agronomists from all over Latin America and twelve from the Near and Middle East are there learning skills to improve the agricultural production of their countries.

The University of Chile has one of the finest programs of advanced economic training in this hemisphere. Of the 57 students enrolled in the Graduate School of Economics, 45 are from outside Chile, and the faculty is rapidly becoming a leading source for highly trained economists throughout Latin America.

Peruvian private initiative has built up the fish meal industry from its inception in 1950 to the point where Peru is now the world's largest exporter of fish meal and stands third only to Communist China and Japan in terms of total production of fish products.

Bolivia has doubled its number of school buildings in the past decade, largely through the efforts of local communities.

Under the Venezuelan land reform program, which began in March, 1960, four million acres have already been distributed to 44,000 families.

In Argentina the Nobel Prize winner, Dr. Bernardo Houssay, after resigning from the University of Buenos Aires in a protest against Peronism, built one of the hemisphere's finest institutes of biology and experimental medicine, relying principally on local subscriptions.

Costa Rica, a country with a population of only 1.2 million, has implemented one of the hemisphere's most successful programs of education. As of now, 240,000 students are enrolled in schools of all types.

Mexico has achieved an increase of 223 per cent in its agricultural production in the last twenty years. Once a large importer of corn and wheat, Mexico has in the last six years become self-sufficient in both crops. The nation has in fact become virtually self-sustaining in the agricultural field.

The Mexican record in the field of public health has been impressive. The anti-malarial campaign which began in 1957, when 25,000 Mexicans were dying each year from malaria, was so effective that in 1960, it is reported, not a single Mexican died from malaria.

These and thousands of other examples serve to illustrate the range and effectiveness which is possible for private and public initiative within a free society. It is, in fact, one of the principal advantages of a free society that it liberates the energy and initiative of thousands of individuals and groups in the service of human welfare.

Second, no real economic development consistent with the goals we have set ourselves is possible without a social structure which permits the great mass of people to share in the benefits of progress, and affords each man a fair expectation of social justice. This often means basic, even revolutionary, changes in the structure of society. Outmoded systems of land tenure which allow a few to hold great estates while most agricultural workers are landless must be swept away. Tax systems which exempt the wealthy from their just share of the burden of development must be revised. And all the institutions of society must be carefully scanned to ensure that they are not instruments for maintaining the privileges of a fortunate few.

Some of these changes are necessary for rational development. But many of them do not find their justification in the calculations of economists or the formulations of planners. They are vital because no government and no nation can carry forward the process of development without the support and help of its people. People will give their assistance only when they are convinced that the government is serving their interest, that they are not being exploited on behalf of a minority, and that they and their children will have fair access to land, jobs, and education. People can be called upon for the sacrifices which development demands when they are convinced that everyone is sharing those sacrifices and that there will be a just distribution of the progress which sacrifice brings.

I am fully aware that these fundamental social reforms are not made without controversy. We are deeply committed to democratic processes and we know from our own experience that economic and social reform involves time, vigorous debate, and the adjustment of contending views. The great human forces which have unleashed the drive for development in the last several years also demand social justice as a part of that development.

The *third* requisite for development is also the most obvious: the human and material resources necessary to permit a nation to build the basic economic structure which will produce long-term growth.

In our rush to create new capital we often neglect the importance of the human resources necessary for economic development. But factories and roads and bridges will not be built without men to plan them, to engineer them, and to manage them. The programming of economic development itself requires the application of a hundred skills; and the implementation of these plans requires thousands of men to run the factories, teach new methods to the farmer and guide the public administration of the developing society. The history of economic progress in all countries is proof that general education, and the development of skills, are the most productive long-run investments which can be made in the future of any nation.

Let me say a word here about the element of time. It is a truism to say that each nation has consumed centuries in getting to where it is today. But in development, decades or even centuries can be jumped over because of the transferability of knowledge and technical skills. We are celebrating the one-hundredth anniversary of our land-grant colleges—but that does not mean that it will take a hundred years to equal that experience elsewhere. The rapid growth of educational systems and institutions of higher education throughout Latin America in the postwar period has been deeply encouraging and lays a solid base for the training of the manpower needed for national development. It is no accident that sharply increased attention is being given, within the Alliance, to the training of leaders—for people remain the bottlenecks for the accomplishment of great human tasks.

Of course large sums of capital will be needed. Much of it will be mobilized within the developing country. But the United States also accepts its obligation to supply a substantial share of the external assistance needed for the success of the Alliance for Progress. These funds can come from only one source—the ordinary taxpayers of the United States; we have no magic mountains of gold. The Alliance is for us a people's effort, just as it is in the rest of the hemisphere. President Kennedy has pledged us to a mammoth ten-year effort, and we intend to live up to that pledge.

With the fulfillment of these three conditions, and with unremitting effort by all of us, we can ensure the success of the Alliance for Progress. And with these same instruments we can also help bring a better life to men and women in other parts of the world.

A Decade of Impatience

The Alliance for Progress represents an acceptance by all nations of the hemisphere of our common responsibility to create an American civilization where no man is forced to live out his life in hunger or hopeless poverty and where every man can expect a better life for himself and his children.

We in the United States are aware of the fact that in the Alliance for Progress we are in a real sense the junior partners—junior because the effort which we can commit will be considerably less than the efforts which will be committed by all the other participating countries. Of the large sums of capital needed for new investment in the next decade perhaps some 20 per cent will come from external sources, and of that more than half will come from the United States. But there remains the 80 per cent which will be mobilized by the peoples of the countries of Latin America. The sums which we envisage as coming from the United States are equivalent to about two per cent of the gross national product of the Latin American members of the Alliance. What the Latin American countries will put into the purposes of the Alliance is equivalent to about 98 per cent of their GNP. I hope that we in the United States will therefore recognize that we are only the junior partners, and that we will do so in good grace and in good spirit, appreciating the fact that we are working with mature societies which have formidable problems on their hands. They have peoples searching for leadership; they have vast populations to educate; they have great national efforts to mobilize and press forward. We understand these problems, even though many of them seem far away.

Another point of major importance has to do with what may turn out to be the most difficult aspect of our Alliance effort. We are dedicating ourselves to a decade of impatience. That is the meaning of the Alliance for Progress. It is customary for free men to take their deepest common commitments for granted and to exaggerate the importance of their marginal differences. One of our problems, therefore, within the family of the hemisphere, is to discover how to combine a desperate urgency with a kind of common feeling that will preserve the unity and fellowship of the American nations.

We must not expect too much. There will be those who will be discontented with the pace of the effort. Some will think the movement is too slow. There will be a few who think that, from their personal standpoints, the movement is too fast.

Some of us here in North America will be impatient with the rate of progress in some of the countries to the South. Some may be a little disturbed because a neighboring country seems to be moving ahead somewhat more rapidly. There will be difficult negotiations regarding the allocation of resources. As one neighbor helps another, in any one of the dozens of ways in which help can be given, all kinds of problems will inevitably arise.

All these things are true. What they mean is that free peoples are doing business with each other in a common effort through free procedures. Therefore, we shall be debating domestically as well as internationally. We shall be negotiating seriously and hard. We shall be dissatisfied—steadily and continually dissatisfied, I hope, because whatever we do will still leave us the great unfinished business of truly achieving freedom. Our job is to get on with this great Alliance, with a solidarity which our commitment to the peoples of the hemisphere requires, and to keep these marginal differences within bounds.

We approach this task confident of the unparalleled creative power of free societies. We approach it with the knowledge, gained from experience, of what needs to be done to advance the development of the American nations. We approach this task with the same unyielding will which created a civilization out of a wilderness and subdued a continent to the service of freedom.

When we succeed in our Alliance, as we shall, then we will have created on this continent a society where people will be liberated from material bondage in order to pursue unhindered the ceaseless quests of the human mind and heart. In this way the basic goals of the United States and of Latin America will be fulfilled. With this achievement, many will look back in later years and say with pride, "I lived during the Alliance for Progress."

THE CHARTER OF PUNTA DEL ESTE

Establishing an Alliance for Progress
Within the Framework of Operation Pan America

PREAMBLE

We, the American Republics, hereby proclaim our decision to unite in a common effort to bring our people accelerated economic progress and broader social justice within the framework of personal dignity and political liberty.

Almost two hundred years ago we began in this Hemisphere the long struggle for freedom which now inspires people in all parts of the world. Today, in ancient lands, men moved to hope by the revolutions of our young nations search for liberty. Now we must give a new meaning to that revolutionary heritage. For America stands at a turning point in history. The men and women of our Hemisphere are reaching for the better life which today's skills have placed within their grasp. They are determined for themselves and their children to have decent and ever more abundant lives, to gain access to knowledge and equal opportunity for all, to end those conditions which benefit the few at the expense of the needs and dignity of the many. It is our inescapable task to fulfill these just desires—to demonstrate to the poor and forsaken of our countries, and of all lands, that the creative powers of free men hold the key to their progress and to the progress of future generations. And our certainty of ultimate success rests not alone on our faith in ourselves and in our nations but on the indomitable spirit of free man which has been the heritage of American civilization.

Inspired by these principles, and by the principles of Operation Pan America and the Act of Bogotá, the American Republics hereby resolve to adopt the following program of action to establish and carry forward an Alliance for Progress.

TITLE I

OBJECTIVES OF THE ALLIANCE FOR PROGRESS

It is the purpose of the Alliance for Progress to enlist the full energies of the peoples and governments of the American republics in a great cooperative effort to accelerate the economic and social development of the participating countries of Latin America, so that they may achieve maximum levels of well-being, with equal opportunities for all, in democratic societies adapted to their own needs and desires.

The American republics hereby agree to work toward the achievement of the following fundamental goals in the present decade:

1. To achieve in the participating Latin American countries a substantial and sustained growth of per capita income at a rate designed to attain, at the earliest possible date, levels of income capable of assuring self-sustaining development, and sufficient to make Latin American income levels constantly larger in relation to the levels of the more industrialized nations. In this way the gap between the living standard of Latin America and those of the more developed countries can be narrowed. Similarly, presently existing differences in income levels among the Latin American countries will be reduced by accelerating the development of the relatively less developed countries and granting them maximum priority in the distribution of resources and in international cooperation in general. In evaluating the degree of relative development, account will be taken not only of average levels of real income and gross product per capita, but also of indices of infant mortality, illiteracy, and per capita daily caloric intake.

It is recognized that, in order to reach these objectives within a reasonable time, the rate of economic growth in any country of Latin America should be not less than 2.5 per cent per capita per year, and that each participating country should determine its own growth target in the light of its stage of social and economic evolution, resource endowment, and ability to mobilize national efforts for development.

2. To make the benefits of economic progress available to all citizens of all economic and social groups through a more equitable distribution of national income, raising more rapidly the income and standard of living of the needier sectors of the population, at the same time that a higher proportion of the national product is devoted to investment.

3. To achieve balanced diversification in national economic structures, both regional and functional, making them increasingly free from dependence on the export of a limited number of primary products and the importation of capital goods while attaining stability in the prices of exports or in income derived from exports.

4. To accelerate the process of rational industrialization so as to increase the productivity of the economy as a whole, taking full advantage of the talents and energies of both the private and public sectors, utilizing the natural resources of the country and providing productive and remunerative employment for unemployed or part-time workers. Within this process of industrialization, special attention should be given to the establishment and development of capital-goods industries.

5. To raise greatly the level of agricultural productivity and output and to improve related storage, transportation, and marketing services.

6. To encourage, in accordance with the characteristics of each country, programs of comprehensive agrarian reform leading to the effective transformation, where required, of unjust structures and systems of land tenure and use, with a view to replacing latifundia and dwarf holdings by an equitable system of land tenure so that, with the help of timely and adequate credit, technical assistance and facilities for the marketing and distribution of products, the land will become for the man who works it the basis of his economic stability, the foundation of his increasing welfare, and the guarantee of his freedom and dignity.

7. To eliminate adult illiteracy and by 1970 to assure, as a minimum, access to six years of primary education for each school-age child in Latin America; to modernize and expand vocational, technical, secondary and higher educational and training facilities, to strengthen the capacity for basic and applied research; and to provide the competent personnel required in rapidly-growing societies.

8. To increase life expectancy at birth by a minimum of five years, and to increase the ability to learn and produce, by improving individual and public health. To attain this goal it will be necessary, among other measures, to provide adequate potable water supply and sewage disposal to not less than 70 per cent of the urban and 50 per cent of the rural population; to reduce

the present mortality rate of children less than five years of age by at least one-half; to control the more serious communicable diseases, according to their importance as a cause of sickness, disability, and death; to eradicate those illnesses, especially malaria, for which effective techniques are known; to improve nutrition; to train medical and health personnel to meet at least minimum requirements; to improve basic health services at national and local levels; and to intensify scientific research and apply its results more fully and effectively to the prevention and cure of illness.

9. To increase the construction of low-cost houses for low-income families in order to replace inadequate and deficient housing and to reduce housing shortages; and to provide necessary public services to both urban and rural centers of population.

10. To maintain stable price levels, avoiding inflation or deflation and the consequent social hardships and maldistribution of resources, always bearing in mind the necessity of maintaining an adequate rate of economic growth.

11. To strengthen existing agreements on economic integration, with a view to the ultimate fulfillment of aspirations for a Latin American common market that will expand and diversify trade among the Latin American countries and thus contribute to the economic growth of the region.

12. To develop cooperative programs designed to prevent the harmful effects of excessive fluctuations in the foreign exchange earnings derived from exports of primary products, which are of vital importance to economic and social development; and to adopt the measures necessary to facilitate the access of Latin American exports to international markets.

TITLE II

ECONOMIC AND SOCIAL DEVELOPMENT

Chapter I. Basic Requirements for Economic and Social Development

The American republics recognize that to achieve the foregoing goals it will be necessary:

1. That comprehensive and well-conceived national programs of economic and social development, aimed at the achievement of self-sustaining growth, be carried out in accordance with democratic principles.

2. That national programs of economic and social development be based on the principle of self-help—as established in the Act of Bogotá—and on the maximum use of domestic resources, taking into account the special conditions of each country.

3. That in the preparation and execution of plans for economic and social development, women should be placed on an equal footing with men.

4. That the Latin American countries obtain sufficient external financial assistance, a substantial portion of which should be extended on flexible conditions with respect to periods and terms of repayment and forms of utilization, in order to supplement domestic capital formation and reinforce their import capacity; and that, in support of well-conceived programs, which include the necessary structural reforms and measures for the mobilization of internal resources, a supply of capital from all external sources during the coming ten years of at least 20 billion dollars be made available to the Latin American countries,

with priority to the relatively less developed countries. The greater part of this sum should be in public funds.

5. That institutions in both the public and private sectors, including labor organizations, cooperatives, and commercial, industrial, and financial institutions, be strengthened and improved for the increasing and effective use of domestic resources, and that the social reforms necessary to permit a fair distribution of the fruits of economic and social progress be carried out.

Chapter II. National Development Programs

1. Participating Latin American countries agree to introduce or strengthen systems for the preparation, execution, and periodic revision of national programs for economic and social development consistent with the principles, objectives, and requirements contained in this document. Participating Latin American countries should formulate, if possible within the next eighteen months, long-term development programs. Such programs should embrace, according to the characteristics of each country, the elements outlined in the Appendix.

2. National development programs should incorporate self-help efforts directed toward:
    a. Improvement of human resources and widening of opportunities by raising general standards of education and health; improving and extending technical education and professional training with emphasis on science and technology; providing adequate remuneration for work performed, encouraging the talents of managers, entrepreneurs, and wage earners; providing more productive employment for underemployed manpower; establishing effective systems of labor relations, and procedures for consultation and collaboration among public authorities, employer associations, and labor organizations; promoting the establishment and expansion of local institutions for basic and applied research; and improving the standards of public administration.

b. Wider development and more efficient use of natural resources, especially those which are now idle or underutilized, including measures for the processing of raw materials.

c. The strengthening of the agricultural base, progressively extending the benefits of the land to those who work it, and ensuring in countries with Indian populations the integration of these populations into the economic, social, and cultural processes of modern life. To carry out these aims, measures should be adopted among others, to establish or improve, as the case may be, the following services: extension, credit, technical assistance, agricultural research and mechanization; health and education; storage and distribution; cooperatives and farmers' associations; and community development.

d. More effective, rational and equitable mobilization and use of financial resources through the reform of tax structures, including fair and adequate taxation of large incomes and real estate, and the strict application of measures to improve fiscal administration. Development programs should include adaptation of budget expenditures to development needs, measures for the maintenance of price stability, the creation of essential credit facilities at reasonable rates of interest, and the encouragement of private savings.

e. Promotion through appropriate measures, including the signing of agreements for the purpose of reducing or eliminating double taxation, of conditions that will encourage the flow of foreign investments and help to increase the capital resources of participating countries in need of capital.

f. Improvement of systems of distribution and sales in order to make markets more competitive and prevent monopolistic practices.

Chapter III. Immediate and Short-Term Action Measures

1. Recognizing that a number of Latin American countries, despite their best efforts, may require emergency financial assistance, the United States will provide assistance from the funds which are or may be established for such purposes. The United States stands ready to take prompt action on applications for such assistance. Applications relating to existing situations should be submitted within the next 60 days.

2. Participating Latin American countries should, in addition to creating or strengthening machinery for long-term development programming, immediately increase their efforts to accelerate their development by giving special emphasis to the following objectives:

   a. The completion of projects already under way and the initiation of projects for which the basic studies have been made, in order to accelerate their financing and execution.
   b. The implementation of new projects which are designed:
      (1) To meet the most pressing economic and social needs and benefit directly the greatest number of people;
      (2) To concentrate efforts within each country in the less developed or more depressed areas in which particularly serious social problems exist;
      (3) To utilize idle capacity or resources, particularly underemployed manpower; and
      (4) To survey and assess natural resources.
   c. The facilitation of the preparation and execution of long-term programs through measures designed:
      (1) To train teachers, technicians, and specialists;
      (2) To provide accelerated training to workers and farmers;
      (3) To improve basic statistics;
      (4) To establish needed credit and marketing facilities; and
      (5) To improve services and administration.

3. The United States will assist in carrying out these short-term measures with a view to achieving concrete results from the Alliance for Progress at the earliest possible moment. In

THE CHARTER OF PUNTA DEL ESTE   127

connection with the measures set forth above, and in accordance with the statement of President Kennedy, the United States will provide assistance under the Alliance, including assistance for the financing of short-term measures, totalling more than one billion dollars in the year ending March 1962.

Chapter IV. External Assistance in Support of National Development Programs

1. The economic and social development of Latin America will require a large amount of additional public and private financial assistance on the part of capital-exporting countries, including the members of the Development Assistance Group and international lending agencies. The measures provided for in the Act of Bogotá and the new measures provided for in this Charter, are designed to create a framework within which such additional assistance can be provided and effectively utilized.

2. The United States will assist those participating countries whose development programs establish self-help measures and economic and social policies and programs consistent with the goals and principles of this Charter. To supplement the domestic efforts of such countries, the United States is prepared to allocate resources which, along with those anticipated from other external sources, will be of a scope and magnitude adequate to realize the goals envisaged in this Charter. Such assistance will be allocated to both social and economic development and, where appropriate, will take the form of grants or loans on flexible terms and conditions. The participating countries will request the support of other capital-exporting countries and appropriate institutions so that they may provide assistance for the attainment of these objectives.

3. The United States will help in the financing of technical assistance projects proposed by a participating country or by the General Secretariat of the Organization of American States for the purpose of:
    a. Providing experts contracted in agreement with the governments to work under their direction and to assist them

in the preparation of specific investment projects and the strengthening of national mechanisms for preparing projects, using specialized engineering firms where appropriate;

b. Carrying out, pursuant to existing agreements for cooperation among the General Secretariat of the Organization of American States, the Economic Commission for Latin America, and the Inter-American Development Bank, field investigations and studies, including those relating to development problems, the organization of national agencies for the preparation of development programs, agrarian reform and rural development, health, cooperatives, housing, education and professional training, and taxation and tax administration; and

c. Convening meetings of experts and officials on development and related problems.

The governments or above-mentioned organizations should, when appropriate, seek the cooperation of the United Nations and its specialized agencies in the execution of these activities.

4. The participating Latin American countries recognize that each has in varying degree a capacity to assist fellow republics by providing technical and financial assistance. They recognize that this capacity will increase as their economies grow. They therefore affirm their intention to assist fellow republics increasingly as their individual circumstances permit.

Chapter V. Organization and Procedures

1. In order to provide technical assistance for the formulation of development programs, as may be requested by participating nations, the Organization of American States, the Economic Commission for Latin America, and the Inter-American Development Bank will continue and strengthen their agreements for coordination in this field, in order to have available a group of programming experts whose service can be used to facilitate the implementation of this Charter. The participating

THE CHARTER OF PUNTA DEL ESTE 129

countries will also seek an intensification of technical assistance from the specialized agencies of the United Nations for the same purpose.

2. The Inter-American Economic and Social Council, on the joint nomination of the Secretary General of the Organization of American States, the President of the Inter-American Development Bank, and the Executive Secretary of the United Nations Economic Commission for Latin America, will appoint a panel of nine high-level experts, exclusively on the basis of their experience, technical ability, and competence in the various aspects of economic and social development. The experts may be of any nationality, though if of Latin American origin an appropriate geographical distribution will be sought. They will be attached to the Inter-American Economic and Social Council, but will nevertheless enjoy complete autonomy in the performance of their duties. They may not hold any other remunerative position. The appointment of these experts will be for a period of three years, and may be renewed.

3. Each government, if it so wishes, may present its program for economic and social development for consideration by an ad hoc committee, composed of no more than three members drawn from the panel of experts referred to in the preceding paragraph together with an equal number of experts not on the panel. The experts who compose the ad hoc committee will be appointed by the Secretary General of the Organization of American States at the request of the interested government and with its consent.

4. The committee will study the development program, exchange opinions with the interested government as to possible modifications and, with the consent of the government, report its conclusions to the Inter-American Development Bank and to other governments and institutions that may be prepared to extend external financial and technical assistance in connection with the execution of the program.

5. In considering a development program presented to it, the ad hoc committee will examine the consistency of the program

with the principles of the Act of Bogotá and of this Charter, taking into account the elements in the Appendix.

6. The General Secretariat of the Organization of American States will provide the personnel needed by the experts referred to in paragraphs 2 and 3 of this Chapter in order to fulfill their tasks. Such personnel may be employed specifically for this purpose or may be made available from the permanent staffs of the Organization of American States, the Economic Commission for Latin America, and the Inter-American Development Bank, in accordance with the present liaison arrangements between the three organizations. The General Secretariat of the Organization of American States may seek arrangements with the United Nations Secretariat, its specialized agencies and the Inter-American Specialized Organizations, for the temporary assignment of necessary personnel.

7. A government whose development program has been the object of recommendations made by the ad hoc committee with respect to external financing requirements may submit the program to the Inter-American Development Bank so that the Bank may undertake the negotiations required to obtain such financing, including the organization of a consortium of credit institutions and governments disposed to contribute to the continuing and systematic financing, on appropriate terms, of the development program. However, the government will have full freedom to resort through any other channels to all sources of financing, for the purpose of obtaining, in full or in part, the required resources.

The ad hoc committee shall not interfere with the right of each government to formulate its own goals, priorities, and reforms in its national development programs.

The recommendations of the ad hoc committee will be of great importance in determining the distribution of public funds under the Alliance for Progress which contribute to the external financing of such programs. These recommendations shall give special consideration to Title I. 1.

The participating governments will also use their good offices to the end that these recommendations may be accepted as a factor of great importance in the decisions taken, for the same purpose, by inter-American credit institutions, other international credit agencies, and other friendly governments which may be potential sources of capital.

8. The Inter-American Economic and Social Council will review annually the progress achieved in the formulation, national implementation, and international financing of development programs; and will submit to the Council of the Organization of American States such recommendations as it deems pertinent.

APPENDIX

Elements of National Development Programs

1. The establishment of mutually consistent targets to be aimed at over the program period in expanding productive capacity in industry, agriculture, mining, transport, power and communications, and in improving conditions of urban and rural life, including better housing, education, and health.

2. The assignment of priorities and the description of methods to achieve the targets, including specific measures and major projects. Specific development projects should be justified in terms of their relative costs and benefits, including their contribution to social productivity.

3. The measures which will be adopted to direct the operations of the public sector and to encourage private action in support of the development program.

4. The estimated cost, in national and foreign currency, of major projects and of the development program as a whole, year by year over the program period.

5. The internal resources, public and private, estimated to become available for the execution of the programs.

6. The direct and indirect effects of the program on the balance of payments, and the external financing, public and private, estimated to be required for the execution of the program.

7. The basic fiscal and monetary policies to be followed in order to permit implementation of the program within a framework of price stability.

8. The machinery of public administration—including relationships with local governments, decentralized agencies and nongovernmental organizations, such as labor organizations, cooperatives, business and industrial organizations—to be used in carrying out the program, adapting it to changing circumstances and evaluating the progress made.

TITLE III

ECONOMIC INTEGRATION OF LATIN AMERICA

The American republics consider that the broadening of present national markets in Latin America is essential to accelerate the process of economic development in the Hemisphere. It is also an appropriate means for obtaining greater productivity through specialized and complementary industrial production which will, in turn, facilitate the attainment of greater social benefits for the inhabitants of the various regions of Latin America. The broadening of markets will also make possible the better use of resources under the Alliance for Progress. Consequently, the American republics recognize that:

1. The Montevideo Treaty (because of its flexibility and because it is open to the adherence of all of the Latin American nations) and the Central American Treaty on Economic Integration are appropriate instruments for the attainment of these objectives, as was recognized in Resolution No. 11 (III) of the Ninth Session of the Economic Commission for Latin America.

2. The integration process can be intensified and accelerated not only by the specialization resulting from the broadening of markets through the liberalization of trade but also through the use of such instruments as the agreements for complementary production within economic sectors provided for in the Montevideo Treaty.

3. In order to insure the balanced and complementary economic expansion of all of the countries involved, the integration process should take into account, on a flexible basis, the condition of countries at a relatively less advanced stage of economic development, permitting them to be granted special, fair, and equitable treatment.

4. In order to facilitate economic integration in Latin America, it is advisable to establish effective relationships between the Latin American Free Trade Association and the group of countries adhering to the Central American Economic Integration Treaty, as well as between either of these groups and other Latin American countries. These arrangements should be established within the limits determined by these instruments.

5. The Latin American countries should coordinate their actions to meet the unfavorable treatment accorded to their foreign trade in world markets, particularly that resulting from certain restrictive and discriminatory policies of extracontinental countries and economic groups.

6. In the application of resources under the Alliance for Progress, special attention should be given not only to investments for multinational projects that will contribute to strengthening the integration process in all its aspects, but also to the necessary

financing of industrial production, and to the growing expansion of trade in industrial products within Latin America.

7. In order to facilitate the participation of countries at a relatively low stage of economic development in multinational Latin American economic cooperation programs, and in order to promote the balanced and harmonious development of the Latin American integration process, special attention should be given to the needs of these countries in the administration of financial resources provided under the Alliance for Progress, particularly in connection with infrastructure programs and the promotion of new lines of production.

8. The economic integration process implies a need for additional investment in various fields of economic activity and funds provided under the Alliance for Progress should cover these needs as well as those required for the financing of national development programs.

9. When groups of Latin American countries have their own institutions for financing economic integration, the financing referred to in the preceding paragraph should preferably be channeled through these institutions. With respect to regional financing designed to further the purposes of existing regional integration instruments, the cooperation of the Inter-American Development Bank should be sought in channeling extra-regional contributions which may be granted for these purposes.

10. One of the possible means for making effective a policy for the financing of Latin American integration would be to approach the International Monetary Fund and other financial sources with a view to providing a means for solving temporary balance-of-payments problems that may occur in countries participating in economic integration arrangements.

11. The promotion and coordination of transportation and communications systems is an effective way to accelerate the integration process. In order to counteract abusive practices in relation to freight rates and tariffs, it is advisable to encourage the establishment of multinational transport and communication

enterprises in the Latin American countries, or to find other appropriate solutions.

12. In working toward economic integration and complementary economies, efforts should be made to achieve an appropriate coordination of national plans, or to engage in joint planning for various economies through the existing regional integration organizations. Efforts should also be made to promote an investment policy directed to the progressive elimination of unequal growth rates in the different geographic areas, particularly in the case of countries which are relatively less developed.

13. It is necessary to promote the development of national Latin American enterprises, in order that they may compete on an equal footing with foreign enterprises.

14. The active participation of the private sector is essential to economic integration and development, and except in those countries in which free enterprise does not exist, development planning by the pertinent national public agencies, far from hindering such participation, can facilitate and guide it, thus opening new perspectives for the benefit of the community.

15. As the countries of the Hemisphere still under colonial domination achieve their independence, they should be invited to participate in Latin American economic integration programs.

TITLE IV

BASIC EXPORT COMMODITIES

The American republics recognize that the economic development of Latin America requires expansion of its trade, a simultaneous and corresponding increase in foreign exchange incomes received from exports, a lessening of cyclical or seasonal fluctuations in the incomes of those countries that still depend heavily on the export of raw materials, and the correction of the secular deterioration in their terms of trade.

They therefore agree that the following measures should be taken:

Chapter I. National Measures

National measures affecting commerce in primary products should be directed and applied in order to:

1. Avoid undue obstacles to the expansion of trade in these products;

2. Avoid market instability;

3. Improve the efficiency of international plans and mechanisms for stabilization; and

4. Increase their present markets and expand their area of trade at a rate compatible with rapid development.

Therefore:

A. Importing member countries should reduce and if possible eliminate, as soon as feasible, all restrictions and discriminatory practices affecting the consumption and importation of primary products, including those with the highest possible degree of processing in the country of origin, except when these restrictions are imposed temporarily for purposes of economic diversification, to hasten the economic development of less developed nations, or to establish basic national reserves. Importing countries should also be ready to support, by adequate regulations, stabilization programs for primary products that may be agreed upon with producing countries.

B. Industrialized countries should give special attention to the need for hastening economic development of less developed countries. Therefore, they should make maximum efforts to create conditions, compatible with their international obligations, through which they may extend advantages to less developed countries so as to permit the rapid expansion of their markets. In view of the great need for this rapid development, industrialized countries should also study ways in which to modify, wherever possible, international commitments which prevent the achievement of this objective.

C. Producing member countries should formulate their plans for production and export, taking account of their effect on world markets and of the necessity of supporting and improving the effectiveness of international stabilization programs and mechanisms. Similarly they should try to avoid increasing the uneconomic production of goods which can be obtained under better conditions in the less developed countries of the Continent, in which the production of these goods is an important source of employment.

D. Member countries should adopt all necessary measures to direct technological studies toward finding new uses and by-products of those primary commodities that are most important to their economies.

E. Member countries should try to reduce, and, if possible, eliminate within a reasonable time export subsidies and other measures which cause instability in the markets for basic commodities and excessive fluctuations in prices and income.

Chapter II. International Cooperation Measures

1. Member countries should make coordinated, and if possible, joint efforts designed:

a. To eliminate as soon as possible undue protection of the production of basic products.
b. To eliminate taxes and reduce excessive domestic prices which discourage the consumption of imported basic products;

c. To seek to end preferential agreements and other measures which limit world consumption of Latin American basic products and their access to international markets, especially the markets of Western European countries in process of economic integration, and of countries with centrally planned economies; and
d. To adopt the necessary consultation mechanisms so that their marketing policies will not have damaging effects on the stability of the markets for basic commodities.

2. Industrialized countries should give maximum cooperation to less developed countries so that their raw material exports will have undergone the greatest degree of processing that is economic.

3. Through their representation in international financial organizations, member countries should suggest that these organizations, when considering loans for the promotion of production for export, take into account the effect of such loans on products which are in surplus in world markets.

4.. Member countries should support the efforts being made by international commodity study groups and by the Commission on International Commodity Trade of the United Nations. In this connection, it should be considered that producing and consuming nations bear a joint responsibility for taking national and international steps to reduce market instability.

5. The Secretary General of the Organization of American States shall convene a group of experts appointed by their respective governments to meet before November 30, 1961 and to report, not later than March 31, 1962 on measures to provide an adequate and effective means of offsetting the effects of fluctuations in the volume and prices of exports of basic products. The experts shall:

a. Consider the questions regarding compensatory financing raised during the present meeting;
b. Analyze the proposal for establishing an international fund for the stabilization of export receipts contained in

the Report of the Group of Experts to the Special Meeting of the Inter-American Economic and Social Council, as well as any other alternative proposals;
c. Prepare a draft plan for the creation of mechanisms for compensatory financing. This draft plan should be circulated among the member Governments and their opinions obtained well in advance of the next meeting of the Commission on International Commodity Trade.

6. Member countries should support the efforts under way to improve and strengthen international commodity agreements and should be prepared to cooperate in the solution of specific commodity problems. Furthermore, they should endeavor to adopt adequate solutions for the short- and long-term problems affecting markets for such commodities so that the economic interests of producers and consumers are equally safeguarded.

7. Member countries should request other producer and consumer countries to cooperate in stabilization programs, bearing in mind that the raw materials of the Western Hemisphere are also produced and consumed in other parts of the world.

8. Member countries recognize that the disposal of accumulated reserves and surpluses can be a means of achieving the goals outlined in the first chapter of this Title, provided that, along with the generation of local resources, the consumption of essential products in the receiving countries is immediately increased. The disposal of surpluses and reserves should be carried out in an orderly manner, in order to:

a. Avoid disturbing existing commercial markets in member countries, and
b. Encourage expansion of the sale of their products to other markets.

However, it is recognized that:

a. The disposal of surpluses should not displace commercial sales of identical products traditionally carried out by other countries; and

b. Such disposal cannot substitute for large scale financial and technical assistance programs.

IN WITNESS WHEREOF this Charter is signed, in Punta del Este, Uruguay, on the seventeenth day of August, nineteen hundred sixty-one.

The original texts shall be deposited in the archives of the Pan American Union, through the Secretary General of the Special Meeting, in order that certified copies may be sent to the Governments of the Member States of the Organization of American States.

(Printed below are the names of the signatories)

FOR VENEZUELA:
  Lorenzo Fernández
  Manuel Pérez Guerrero
  José Antonio Mayobre
  Mercedes Carvajal de Arocha
  Daniel Orellana
  Virgilio Fernández

FOR GUATEMALA:
  Joaquín Prieto Barrios
  Julio Prado García Salas
  Alberto Arreaga

FOR BOLIVIA:
  Alfonso Gumucio Reyes

FOR MEXICO:
  Antonio Ortiz Mena

FOR THE DOMINICAN REPUBLIC:
  Salvador Ortiz

FOR COLOMBIA:
  Hernando Agudelo Villa
  Carlos Sanz de Santamaría
  José Joaquín Gori
  Santiago Salazar Santos
  Gabriel Betancur Mejía

FOR ARGENTINA:
  Roberto T. Alemann

FOR PERU:
  Pedro Beltrán
  Gonzalo N. de Aramburú

FOR ECUADOR:
  Jaime Nebot Velasco
  Joaquín Zevallos Menéndez
  Fernando Manrique
  Atahualpa Chávez González
  Julio Prado Vallejo

THE CHARTER OF PUNTA DEL ESTE

FOR PARAGUAY:
Ezequiel González Alsina
José A. Moreno González
César Romeo Acosta
Julio C. Gutiérrez

FOR HONDURAS:
Jorge Bueso Arias
Roberto Ramírez
Carlos H. Matute
Lempira Bonilla

FOR PANAMA:
Gilberto Arias
Jorge R. Riba
Carlos Malgrat

FOR HAITI:
Vilfort Beauvoir
Gerard Phillipeaux
Henri Marc Charles

FOR COSTA RICA:
Manuel G. Escalante
Manuel Enrique Herrero
Antonio Orlich
Antonio Cañas
Mariano S. Sanz

FOR THE UNITED STATES OF AMERICA:
Douglas Dillon
Robert F. Woodward

FOR URUGUAY:
Juan Eduardo Azzini
Homero Martínez Montero
Nicolás Storace Arrosa
Modesto Rebollo
Héctor Lorenzo y Losada

FOR EL SALVADOR:
Manuel Francisco Chavarría
Víctor Manuel Cuéllar Ortiz
Francisco Monterrosa Gavidia
Luis Montenegro

FOR CHILE:
Eduardo Figueroa

FOR CUBA:

FOR NICARAGUA:
Juan José Lugo Marenco
Carlos J. C. H. Hueck
Guillermo Sevilla Sacasa
Francisco Urcuyo
Nasere Habed López

FOR BRAZIL:
Clemente Mariani Bittencourt
Arthur Bernardes Filho
E. P. Barbosa da Silva
Roberto de Oliveira Campos

INDEX

A

Act of Bogotá, 1, 2, 12, 14, 23, 90; see also Bogotá
Agricultural technology, 38–41; see also Technology
Agriculture, 8, 38–43, 65, 97
Aid, U.S. to Latin America:
conditions of 11, 12, 15, 18, 62, 94, 114;
emergency aid needed, 72–73;
importance of, 50–51;
initiation of, 9
Alliance for Progress:
economic shortcomings of, 72;
establishment of, 16, 90;
goals of, 16, 17;
Latin American genesis of, 24–26
Allocation of Latin American resources, 50–51, 57–61, 91–92, 116; see also Resources
Argentina, 78, 112

B

Batista, Fulgencio, 19, 94
Betancourt, Romulo, 79
Bogotá:
Act of, 1, 2, 12, 14, 23, 90;
Committee of Twenty-one of OAS (1960), meeting of, 13, 14, 18, 90
Bolivar, Simon, 70, 104
Bolivia, 63, 111
Brazil, 79

C

Capital:
accumulation, 28, 29, 30, 46–50, 77;
flight of, 92;
mobilization of, 114–15
Capital, foreign private:
need for, 8, 50, 51, 53, 114–15;
role of, 10, 37, 56–57;
U.S., 6, 8, 10–11
Castro, Fidel, 2, 12, 18, 19, 20
Castro-Communism, 18–19, 20, 23
Chapultepec, Act of, 7
Chile, University of, 111
Chilean Student Federation, 21–22
Coffee:
agreements, 74;
stabilization plan, 10;
see also Commodities, primary
Colombia, 78
Colombian Technical Institute, 111
Commissions to Promote Inter-American Understanding, 2
Committee of Twenty-one of OAS. See under Bogotá and Organization of American States
Commodities, primary:
export of, 8, 10, 27, 32, 76;
International Commodity Fund, need for, 74;
stabilization of, 12;
study groups, 10
Common Market, Latin American, 12, 19, 25, 33–38
Communism, 20, 21, 22, 23:
in Costa Rica, 68, 87;

INDEX

in Cuba, 2, 18, 19–20, 68, 87;
in Guatemala, 68, 87;
struggle against, 66–69, 86–87, 103–106
Communist bloc, lack of economic growth in, 107–109
Conditions for aid. *See under* Aid, U.S. to Latin America
Congress, U.S., 13, 14
Costa Rica:
Communism in, 68, 87;
dependence on exports, 76;
economic conditions in, 79;
education in, 112;
taxation in, 77
Cuba:
Communism in, 2, 18, 19–20, 68, 87;
dissents from Act of Bogotá, 14;
excluded from OAS, 18;
nationalization of U.S. investments, 19;
revolution in, 20, 68, 94;
U.S. intervention in, 4–5

D

Declaration to the Peoples of America, 16; *see also* Punta del Este
Development policies, 31; *see also* Planning, economic

E

Economic Commission for Latin America (ECLA), Common Market Working Group, 35
Economic development, 26 ff.:
importance of education to, 98–99;
role of individuals in, 30;
see also Planning, s.v. economic
Ecuador, 79
Education:
goals for, 99–101;
growth of higher, 111–12, 114;
importance to development, 98–99;
need for reforms in, 8, 9, 14;
primary and secondary, 45
Emergency aid, 72–73; *see also* Aid, U.S. to Latin America
European customs, intellectual revolt against, 4
European investment in Latin America, 4
Export-Import Bank, 9
Export of primary commodities, 8, 10, 27, 32, 76
Exports, Latin American:
dependence on, 74–76;
to Europe, 8;
policies toward, 31–33

F

Foreign Investment, 50–51, 54–57, 61–62; *see also* Investment
Foreign private capital. *See* Capital, foreign private
Foreign private enterprise, role of, 7, 29, 53–56; *see also* Private enterprise
Foreign resources, 50–51, 61–62, 115; *see also* Resources
Friends of the United States of Latin America (FUSLA), 82

G

Goals of the Alliance for Progress, 16, 19
Good Neighbor Policy, 6, 7, 9
Gross national product, Latin American nations, 115
Guatemala, Communism in, 68, 87

H

Health, public, need for improvement in, 8, 9, 14, 92
Housing, need for improvement in, 8, 9, 14, 92
Houssay, Bernardo, 112
Human resources, 44–45, 99–100, 113–15; *see also* Resources

I

Imports, Latin American, 27; restrictions on, 32, 33
Income, per capita in Latin America, 10, 30
Industrialization:
  need for, 24, 27–28
  policies toward, 31–33
Inter-American Association for Democracy and Freedom, 82
Inter-American Development Bank:
  establishment of, 14
  need for, 11, 12
Inter-American Institute of Political Education, 83
Inter-American Treaty of Reciprocal Assistance (Rio Treaty), 7
Inter-American understanding, need for, 2, 68, 69
International Commodity Fund, need for, 74
International Monetary Fund, 74
Intervention, U.S., 4–5, 6, 11, 15
Investment:
  foreign, 50–51, 54–57, 61–62;
  programs, 63;
  ratio between forms of, 30;
  social and productive, 59–60

K

Kennedy, John F., 26, 83, 114
Keynes, Maynard, 74

L

Labor, 11, 28, 29, 33, 60, 98:
  unions, 47;
  U.S., 82;
  see also Manpower
Land:
  reform, 11, 13, 24, 41–43, 65, 97, 111;
  taxation, 13;
  tenure, 13, 38–39, 65, 112–13
Lastarria, Jose Victorino, 4

Latin American Free Trade Association, 34; see also Common Market
Latin American Institute of Economic and Social Development, 100
Loans, conditions for obtaining, 11; see also Export-Import Bank

M

Manpower:
  surplus, 41–43, 100–101;
  use of, 28, 29, 30, 60, 114;
  see also Labor
Marshall Plan, 8, 72, 79
Mexico:
  agricultural production in, 112;
  economic growth of, 78;
  Ministry of Agriculture, 111
  oil holdings expropriated by, 7;
  public health in, 112;
  revolution in, 20;
  U.S. intervention in, 4, 5
Mill, John Stuart, 45
Misunderstanding in hemisphere, causes of, 66, 67; see also Inter-American Understanding
Mobilization of capital. See under Capital
Monroe, James, 3
Monroe Doctrine, 5, 6
Montevideo, Treaty of, 34
Morrow, Dwight, 6
Movement of population. See under Population

N

National income, distribution of, 13
Nationalization of U.S. investments in Cuba, 19
Neglect of Latin American private enterprise. See under Private Enterprise

INDEX

O

Organization of American States (OAS):
Charter of, 7
committee of Twenty-one of, 12, 13
Cuba excluded from, 18, 22
panel of high level experts, 91

Charter of, 1, 2, 23, 24, 25, 90, 94; text, 118-41;
Declaration to the Peoples of America, 16;
meeting of foreign ministers (1962), 18, 22;
ministerial meeting of IA-ECOSOC, 16, 23, 24, 90

P

Panel of high level experts. *See under* Organization of American States
Peace Corps, 94
Perez Jimenez, Marcos, 18, 94
Peron, Juan Domingo, 18
Peru, 78, 111
Planning:
economic, 12, 25, 31-33, 57-62, 71-75, 92;
social, 91-92
Platt Amendment, 5
Policies toward exports. *See under* Exports
Policies toward industrialization. *See under* Industrialization
Political parties, 81-83
Population:
agricultural, 39-40;
dynamic elements of, 30;
increase in, 28;
movement of, 97
Porter, Charles O., 71
Private enterprise:
neglect of Latin American, 73-74;
potentialities of Latin American 54-56;
role of foreign, 7, 29, 53-56
Productive investment, 59-60; *see also* Investment
Protectionism, economic:
Latin American, 27, 33-37;
U.S. 7, 27
Punta del Este:

R

Ratio between forms of investment, 30; *see also* Investment
Raw materials, 27, 33
Reforms, need for, 8, 9, 14, 92; *see also* Social reforms
Resources:
foreign, 50-51, 61-62, 115;
human, 44-45, 99-100, 113-15;
use and allocation of Latin American, 50-41, 57-61, 91-92, 116;
see also Commodities
Restrictions on imports, 32, 33
Revolution in Cuba. *See under* Cuba
Rio Treaty of Reciprocal Assistance, 7
Roosevelt, Franklin D., 26

S

San Martin, Jose de, 104
Sarmiento, Domingo Faustino, 4
Social investment. *see under* Investment
Social justice, 3, 10, 11, 13, 65, 75-76, 93-95, 112; *see also* Social reforms
Social reforms, 10, 13, 15, 19, 24, 26, 52-53, 64-65, 75-77, 92, 95-96, 112-13; *see also* Social justice
Stabilization of commodities. *See under* Commodities, primary

Surplus manpower. *See under* Manpower
Synthetic materials, 27

T

Tariffs, U. S.:
Acts of 1920 and 1930, 6; adjustments of, 7
Taxation, 11, 48, 52, 77, 112–13
Technical assistance, 9, 54–56
Technical training, 36–37, 43–45, 98
Technology:
agricultural, 38–41; assimilation of modern, 26–29; diffusion of, 56–57, 105–106
Trade, Latin American with U.S., 8, 9; *see also* Common Market
Trujillo, Rafael Leonidas, 18

U

United Nations, 9
United States foreign policy, goals of, 102–106
United States labor, 82
United States private capital, 6–8, 10–11; *see also* Capital, Foreign private
United States Public Law, 735, 14

V

Venezuela, 79, 111

W

Walker, William, 4
Washington, George, 104